JESUS
According to Luke

DATE DUE

JESUS
According to Luke

✳ WILLIAM SYDNOR

The Seabury Press / New York

To
Carrie and Buck and Carole
who have taken seriously the call to
witness to the ends of the earth

1982
The Seabury Press
815 Second Avenue
New York, N.Y. 10017

Scripture quotations contained in the text are from the *Revised
Standard Version of the Bible*, copyright © 1946, 1952,
New Testament Section, Second Edition, copyright © 1971,
by the Division of Christian Education of the National Council
of the Churches of Christ in the United States of America.

Library of Congress Cataloging in Publication Data
Sydnor, William.   Jesus according to Luke.
Bibliography: p. 135
1. Bible. N.T. Luke—Criticism, interpretation, etc.
I. Title   BS2595.2.S92   226'.4077   82-3293
ISBN O-8164-2393-8   AACR2

CONTENTS

PREFACE

All Christians, when they become members of some branch of the Church, answer these two questions:

Do you accept Jesus Christ as your Savior?

Do you promise to follow and obey him as your Lord?

They may do this in a formal, liturgical service or in one that is as informal as a river-bank baptism. But it happens; that decisive "I do" is called forth.

We come to a knowledge of what it means to call Jesus Christ Lord and Savior perhaps in part from being impressed by the Christ-likeness of some individual, but certainly through reading the gospels and meditating upon them. There is, however, much in each of the gospels that we may find difficult to understand, and we need help to appreciate the details, nuances, and implications. That is what I have tried to do here—provide the help which will enable us to read Luke's Gospel with greater understanding.

The treatment throughout has been first to provide readers with enough in-hand information so that they can read the Lucan passage with some intelligence and appreciation. Then follows the actual Lucan text, and, where it is thought to be helpful, a follow-up comment which seeks to throw light on the significance of the passage just read.

I have avoided footnotes and scholarly quotations in an effort to make the presentation as simple and direct as possible, but, of course, I have leaned heavily on the writings of a host of New

Testament scholars, especially those whose works are listed in the bibliography.

I am thankful that my wife, Caroline, understands from experience the discipline under which one lives while trying to find the appropriate words to express one's thoughts. She has been of more help than she realizes. The Rev. Dr. Reginald H. Fuller and Christian Hoven both read the manuscript and made helpful suggestions and gentle criticisms for which I am most grateful, but responsibility for the interpretive comments throughout is entirely mine.

February 10, 1982   *William Sydnor*

CHAPTER 1

WHAT YOU NEED
TO KNOW FIRST

This book is intended to lead you into a deeper appreciation of Luke's Gospel. In order to find a New Testament gospel intelligible one needs to be quite clear as to what a piece of writing called "a gospel" is. Only thus are we defended from having the wrong expectations from our perusal of the Gospel according to Luke.

The Greek word *Evaggelion* means good news. It comes into English via two routes. By transliteration it is lifted over into English as "evangel" and the writer of a gospel is an evangelist. It was also translated into Old English — godspell — which in time became "gospel."

An evangelist is not a court reporter nor is he a newspaper correspondent sending out wire dispatches from the scene. He is recording the good news about Jesus Christ *as he understands it*. He uses the materials which have come to him in the way and in the order in which they will enhance, explain, and convince the reader of the wonderful news contained in the life and teachings, the death and resurrection of Jesus Christ.

Luke the evangelist is usually referred to as a historian. If writing history is merely giving events in chronological order, Luke fails the test. But if one takes a less rigid view and agrees that the writing of history may properly include not only an interpretive function (which all history writing does, intentionally or not) but also a thematic presentation of material, Luke deserves the title.

Luke was a second-generation Christian, probably from the vicinity of Antioch. He was a physician and a close friend of Paul the Apostle and traveled with him during his most strenuous journeys. Luke may have been a Greek, and he was certainly well-versed in the Greek Old Testament as well as in the ways of the synagogue. He was artistic, something of a poet, and was gifted in depicting the people who cross the pages of his Gospel. Indeed his main interest is in people, not ideas. He has a keen social consciousness and a boundless sympathy for all kinds of people in their troubles and difficulties. Think, then, of Luke as a kindly, gifted, scholarly man.

He wrote two books — the Gospel according to Luke and the Acts of the Apostles — which together comprise nearly one-fourth of the New Testament. Here is the preface of his first book, the Gospel:

1:1–4

Inasmuch as many have undertaken to compile a narrative of the things which have been accomplished among us, 2 just as they were delivered to us by those who from the beginning were eyewitnesses and ministers of the word, 3 it seemed good to me also, having followed all things closely for some time past, to write an orderly account for you, most excellent Theophilus, 4 that you may know the truth concerning the things of which you have been informed.

Thus Luke tells us why he wrote his Gospel and where he got his information. He addresses it to "most excellent Theophilus," a Roman official, but I think that is a screen. Luke was writing around 80 to 85 A.D., fifty years or so after the crucifixion-resurrection and a short decade or two after the Emperor Nero's barbarous persecution of Christians. No Roman official would have taken the time or bothered to risk an interest in Christianity. It is more probable that the name Theophilus, meaning "Beloved of God," was the pseudonym for a confessing Christian and was used to protect him from the perils of persecution. And when we get into Luke's Gospel we feel certain that "Theophilus" was not the only intended reader. Luke is addressing the Church of his day and dealing with the issues important to that Church.

Among those issues are the accusations being leveled at the Christian Church and its members. Here are some of them. Christians are all suspect. They are followers of a condemned and crucified criminal. Luke's Gospel makes it clear that the representatives of Roman law considered Jesus innocent. Again: the diverse people of the Roman Empire considered Christianity nothing but a foreign superstition. Not so, says Luke. His Gospel shows it to be the fulfillment of Old Testament predictions and promises, and thus deserving of the same tolerance granted the Jews throughout the empire. But even more, it is not nationalistic like Judaism but is a world religion which can meet the spiritual needs of everyone in the empire and beyond.

Still again: Rome is always suspicious of possible revolt, and these revolutionaries talk of "the kingdom of God" and of "Jesus Christ the king of the Jews." They have a mistaken impression, says Luke. His Gospel makes it clear that Jesus turned his back on political revolution while seeking a deeper revolution of values and point of view. Still another criticism of Christians was that they were suspected of antisocial behavior. Luke counters this by showing throughout his Gospel that Jesus is continually reaching out to all kinds of people and even raising the level of decency and respect for the outcasts of society.

So it is that Luke tells "Theophilus" that he is writing "that you may know the truth concerning the things of which you have been informed." Perhaps what he is really doing is providing the Christians with answers to the questions of their non-Christian neighbors.

Luke collected his material from eyewitnesses, from documents, and from the traditions and practices of the Church. We know of three written sources which he used. The first was Mark's Gospel, composed only recently, since the burning of Rome in 64 A.D. and the persecution of Christians which followed. About fifty-five percent of Mark's actual words are reproduced in Luke. (Matthew also leans heavily on Mark.) His second source is one that he and Matthew both used, material which does not appear in Mark. It has the undistinguished name of "Q" — from the German word *Quelle*, meaning source. And his third source — which contains oral and written materials and traditions — is one which he alone uses; scholars call it "L." Mark and "Q" comprise about half of Luke; the other half comes from "L."

The material in "Q" and "L" is for the most part a miscellany of what Jesus said and did with no indication of chronology. For example, consider Jesus' poignant lament over the Holy City, "O Jerusalem, Jerusalem, killing the prophets and stoning those who are sent to you!" Matthew uses these words as the climax of Jesus' diatribe against the scribes and Pharisees following the Triumphal Entry during his Holy Week discourses (Matt. 23:37-39). Luke uses them much earlier, during Jesus' final journey to Jerusalem and prior to the beginning of Holy Week. Each evangelist arranges his material so as to make clear the significance of the Jesus story as he understands it.

Luke is writing religious history. His Gospel is not primarily biography; it is proclamation. He proclaims the gospel by narrating history rather than by logical argument such as Paul uses in Romans 9-11. And that gospel is that Jesus came in fulfillment of prophecy, that his ministry is the period in which God's promises of salvation are realized. But many of the Jews rejected him; so the Christian Church becomes the fulfillment of Israel's hope, and non-Jews, indeed all peoples, are offered the benefits of God's salvation.

What we have in Luke's Gospel is salvation history, and in telling it he uses miracles as a way of expressing the power and magnitude of the salvation God is disposed to bestow through the person of Jesus of Nazareth. The recipients of this salvation are not the rulers of Israel who are actually responsible for Jesus' condemnation and death; rather, the recipients are the lowly and outcast of society. Luke's Gospel, from beginning to end, is a long procession of such folk — shepherds, women and widows, children, soldiers, sinners, Samaritans, Gentiles, tax-collectors, the poor, the suffering, the oppressed, the sick and afflicted, criminals. It is to the lost in Israel that Jesus brings salvation, and they receive him in faith. Luke raises our consciousness to see God's saving activity being disclosed in Jesus Christ (and later, in Acts, through the Church). This Gospel writer is a careful theologian who in the course of telling the story of the life, death, resurrection, and ascension of Jesus explains, as we shall see, the meaning of the Holy Spirit, the Messiah, suffering, the Kingdom of God, and divine judgment.

We are about to explore a most extraordinary document, written by an extraordinarily gifted person.

CHAPTER 2

IN THE DAYS OF HEROD AND CAESAR AUGUSTUS

Luke's story opens with two beautiful chapters which tell of the birth of John the Baptist and of Jesus. The strange thing is that those chapters could have been omitted — going straight from the Preface (1:1–4) to Chapter Three — and the unknowing reader would not have missed them. Under such a circumstance the beginning of Luke's account would have been like that of Mark with more details. So these two opening chapters need to be examined as a separate unit with their own significance.

When we examine this series of stories with which Luke begins his history we find that at some point almost every character bursts into song. Indeed, these chapters belong more to the realm of poetry than to the prose of a careful historian. What we have here is Luke the artist preparing us to appreciate what happens when spiritual purpose and power break in upon the mundane affairs of the everyday world.

The material Luke used comes from several traditions of remembering and retelling. The hymns attributed to the principal actors appropriately express the significance of the moment in becoming language, too perfect to have been spontaneous. Some scholars surmise that the account of John's birth may have come from the disciples of John the Baptist and that the hymns may have already been in use in worship by some Christians. Most scholars agree that we have to be content to live with the uncertainty as to where fact ends and interpretation begins.

One helpful way to appreciate these chapters is to think of them as a prelude to what follows. The great dramatic musicals which came to the American stage during the middle years of this century—such as "My Fair Lady," "The King and I," and "The Sound of Music"—all began with a prelude. This orchestral number was composed of a blending of bits of melody from a number of the songs which the audience would hear in the course of the show. It provided something of a foretaste, a hint of what was to come later, to whet one's appreciation and anticipation. Luke is doing just that. For instance, look at three examples. (1) The Holy Spirit which is involved with Jesus' birth (1:35) will be the source of his inspiration and power in the days of his ministry (3:22; 4:14). (2) "Of his kingdom there will be no end," said the angel to Mary (1:33), and "the good news of the kingdom" was integral to his preaching from the very first (4:43). (3) The angel's announcement to the shepherds calls Jesus "Savior," "Christ" (Messiah), and "Lord" (2:11) and his life, death, resurrection, and ascension give these titles deep meaning.

Now let us take a closer look at this prelude.

Zechariah's Vision

There had been a time when the Jewish nation was free. But for the past century the Romans had ruled the Jews, taxed them, and governed them through a family of kings called the Herods who were like puppets on a Roman string. There was also a Roman governor in Judea who collected, or procured, the taxes and kept the peace; he was called a *procurator*. The Jews naturally hated their Roman rulers and those who cooperated with them. They believed that God would send a Messiah to deliver them from the Romans.

The prophet had said that the Messiah would suddenly come to his temple. But before his coming Elijah would inaugurate a great time of repentance (Mal. 3:1; 4:4-6). Appropriately, Luke's story about the Messiah begins in the Temple. First we meet Zechariah, a priest. All male descendants of Aaron were entitled to officiate at Temple sacrifices. They were divided into twenty-four divisions each of which served twice a year. The most coveted assignment was to be chosen to enter the sanctuary and burn incense. The rising smoke of the incense was symbolic of the prayers of the people going up to God. The priest then came out of the sanctuary and pronounced God's blessing on the people. Many priests never had this coveted assignment. So the occasion was the greatest day in Zechariah's life. His mind, no doubt, was filled with the messianic longings of his people. And the shadow on his personal life — the fact that he and Elizabeth were childless, which was considered a reproach — this also occupied his mind.

Even though God cannot be seen, vivid religious experience is described in terms of seeing and hearing. God's presence is spoken of as "an angel," God's messenger. Zechariah's encounter is with Gabriel, the angel of revelation, who brings news too good to be believable both to childless Zechariah and Elizabeth, and to the people of Israel. Let Luke tell it.

1:5-25

5 In the days of Herod, king of Judea, there was a priest named Zechariah, of the division of Abijah; and he had a wife of the daughters of Aaron, and her name was Elizabeth. 6 And they were both righteous before God, walking in all the commandments and ordinances of the Lord blameless. 7 But they had no child, because Elizabeth was barren, and both were advanced in years.

8 Now while he was serving as priest before God when his division was on duty, 9 according to the custom of the priesthood, it fell to him by lot to enter the temple of the Lord and burn incense. 10 And the whole multitude of the people were praying outside at the hour of incense. 11 And there appeared to him an angel of the Lord standing on the right side of the altar of incense. 12 And Zechariah was troubled when he saw him, and

fear fell upon him. 13 But the angel said to him, "Do not be afraid, Zechariah, for your prayer is heard, and your wife Elizabeth will bear you a son, and you shall call his name John.

14 And you will have joy and gladness,
and many will rejoice at his birth;
15 for he will be great before the Lord,
and he shall drink no wine nor strong drink,
and he will be filled with the Holy Spirit,
even from his mother's womb.
16 And he will turn many of the sons of Israel to the
   Lord their God,
17 and he will go before him in the spirit and
   power of Elijah,
to turn the hearts of the fathers to the children,
and the disobedient to the wisdom of the just,
to make ready for the Lord a people prepared."

18 And Zechariah said to the angel, "How shall I know this? For I am an old man, and my wife is advanced in years." 19 And the angel answered him, "I am Gabriel, who stand in the presence of God; and I was sent to speak to you, and to bring you this good news. 20 And behold, you will be silent and unable to speak until the day that these things come to pass, because you did not believe my words, which will be fulfilled in their time." 21 And the people were waiting for Zechariah, and they wondered at his delay in the temple. 22 And when he came out, he could not speak to them, and they perceived that he had seen a vision in the temple; and he made signs to them and remained dumb. 23 And when his time of service was ended, he went to his home.

24 After these days his wife Elizabeth conceived, and for five months she hid herself, saying, 25 "Thus the Lord has done to me in the days when he looked on me, to take away my reproach among men."

The Annunciation

The scene shifts. The Angel Gabriel now appears to Mary, Elizabeth's "kinswoman." This is the only suggestion that Jesus and John were blood kin. Other Gospel references suggest that John had never heard of Jesus. This is one of the numerous indications that the material came from different sources.

The people wondered not only when, but how, the Messiah would come. Luke's answer is that he would be born of a woman, that he would enter upon the status of divine sonship at his birth, and that the Holy Spirit which brooded over the waters at creation would be involved in his birth. The angel Gabriel told Mary of the unique divine mission of the son she was to have. This was the reason for her wondering awe.

1:26–56

26 In the sixth month the angel Gabriel was sent from God to a city of Galilee named Nazareth, 27 to a virgin betrothed to a man whose name was Joseph, of the house of David; and the virgin's name was Mary. 28 And he came to her and said, "Hail, O favored one, the Lord is with you!" 29 But she was greatly troubled at the saying, and considered in her mind what sort of greeting this might be. 30 And the angel said to her, "Do not be afraid, Mary, for you have found favor with God. 31 And behold, you will conceive in your womb and bear a son, and you shall call his name Jesus.

32 He will be great, and will be called the Son of
the Most High;
and the Lord God will give to him the throne of his
father David,
33 and he will reign over the house of Jacob forever;
and of his kingdom there will be no end."

34 And Mary said to the angel, "How shall this be, since I have no husband?" 35 And the angel said to her,
"The Holy Spirit will come upon you, and the

power of the Most High will overshadow you;
therefore the child to be born will be called holy,
the Son of God.

36 And behold, your kinswoman Elizabeth in her old
age has also conceived a son; and this is the sixth month
with her who was called barren. 37 For with God nothing will be impossible." 38 And Mary said, "Behold I
am the handmaid of the Lord; let it be to me according
to your word." And the angel departed from her.

39 In those days Mary arose and went with haste into
the hill country, to a city of Judah, 40 and she entered
the house of Zechariah and greeted Elizabeth. 41 And
when Elizabeth heard the greeting of Mary, the babe
leaped in her womb; and Elizabeth was filled with the
Holy Spirit 42 and she exclaimed with a loud cry,
"Blessed you among women, and blessed is the fruit of
your womb! 43 And why is this granted me, that the
mother of my Lord should come to me? 44 For behold,
when the voice of your greeting came to my ears, the
babe in my womb leaped for joy. 45 And blessed is she
who believed that there would be a fulfillment of what
was spoken to her from the Lord." 46 And Mary said,

"My soul magnifies the Lord,

47 and my spirit rejoices in God my savior,

48 for he has regarded the low estate of his hand-
maiden.

For behold, henceforth all generations will call me
blessed;

49 for he who is mighty has done great things for
me, and holy is his name.

50 And his mercy is on those who fear him
from generation to generation.

51 He has shown strength with his arm,
he has scattered the proud in the imagination of
their hearts,

52 he has put down the mighty from their thrones,

and exalted those of low degree;
53 he has filled the hungry with good things,
and the rich he has sent empty away.
54 He has helped his servant Israel,
in remembrance of his mercy,
55 as he spoke to our fathers,
to Abraham and to his posterity forever."
56 And Mary remained with her about three months,
and returned to her home.

This beautiful passage is the source of much great art on canvas and in music. It is also a focal point regarding belief in the Virgin Birth. Scholars agree that Luke had source materials which he edited to accommodate the scheme of his Gospel. Whether his original materials represent the Church's attempt to express the great significance of Jesus or whether a historic event lies behind the words is not known. Unquestionably Matthew believed in the virginal conception of Jesus and Luke seems to have, although he limits his view to two mild hints (1:34 and 3:23). At the same time he does not hesitate to call Joseph Jesus' parent (2:33, 41, 43, 48) and have Gabriel proclaim that he will have "the throne of his father David," a messianic identity in part proven by his lineal descent from David through Joseph (3:23; see also 18:38; 20:41). The problem here is that Luke is striving to express the ineffable in human terms. It is not surprising if human language breaks down under the strain and recourse is made to the language of symbolism.

Of course those who believe the Virgin Birth is simple history must believe that the story came ultimately from Mary herself — a beautiful, awesome, treasured part of Christian heritage. But there are also those who find this belief an impediment to faith. To support this latter view is the fact that neither Mark, the earliest Gospel, nor Paul, whose Epistles antedate the Gospels, make any reference to it. Paul unquestionably believed in the divinity of Christ, and Mark's Gospel is about "Jesus Christ the Son of God" (1:1). Either they did not know about the Virgin

Birth or they did not think it was important. The fact is that the story does not seem to have influenced early Christian thinking about Jesus. This would suggest that it was not known because it was not developed until a later date.

What we have in the annunciation of the angel to Mary is Luke's view, based on tradition, of how the birth of Jesus is to be understood. The account shrouds the event in mystery but one thing is clear: the son of Mary is the Son of God, the long-promised Messiah.

Let it be recognized that the pivotal Christian belief is the resurrection of our Lord, not the Virgin Birth. From the earliest moments of Christian preaching and writing Jesus Christ the Lord has been recognized as "Son of God in power according to the Spirit of holiness by his resurrection from the dead" (Rom. 1:4). So whether the Virgin Birth is fact or symbol it remains a precious and beautiful part of the heritage of all who believe in the Risen Lord. We are indebted to Luke for the story of the annunciation, which — like raindrops on a rose — is to be viewed with appreciation, not subjected to the rough hands of angry argument.

The Birth of John the Baptist

The story of John's birth and of his father's miraculously restored speech form a backdrop for Zechariah's hymn, *Benedictus*. It is easy to see how Luke's slight editing could have transformed an early Christian hymn about Jesus Christ into Zechariah's foretelling of the role of his son, John the Baptist, in relation to the Christ.

1:57–69

57 Now the time came for Elizabeth to be delivered, and she gave birth to a son. 58 And her neighbors and kinsfolk heard that the Lord has shown great mercy to her, and they rejoiced with her. 59 And on the eighth

day they came to circumcise the child; and they would
have named him Zechariah after his father, 60 but his
mother said, "Not so; he shall be called John." 61 And
they said to her, "None of your kindred is called by this
name." 62 And they made signs to his father, inquiring
what he would have him called. 63 And he asked for a
writing tablet, and wrote, "His name is John." And they
all marveled. 64 And immediately his mouth was opened
and his tongue loosed, and he spoke, blessing God. 65
And fear came on all their neighbors. And all these
things were talked about through all the hill country of
Judea; 66 and all who heard them laid them up in their
hearts, saying, "What then will this child be?" For the
hand of the Lord was with him.

67 And his father Zechariah was filled with the Holy
Spirit and prophesied, saying,

> 68 "Blessed be the Lord God of Israel,
> for he has visited and redeemed his people,
> 69 and has raised up a horn of salvation for us
> in the house of his servant David . . . .

1:76–80

> 76 And you, child, will be called the prophet of the
>   Most High;
> for you will go before the Lord to prepare his ways,
> 77 to give knowledge of salvation to his people
> in the forgiveness of their sins,
> 78 through the tender mercy of our God,
> when the day shall dawn upon us from on high
> 79 to give light to those who sit in darkness and in
>   the shadow of death,
> to guide our feet into the way of peace."

80 And the child grew and became strong in spirit, and
he was in the wilderness till the day of his manifestation
to Israel.

The Birth of Jesus

Now we come to the birth of Jesus. The exquisite beauty of the account is a blending of prophecy, history, and symbolism which cannot be successfully separated. It belongs properly in the realm of poetry, worship, and awe, not in the cold climate of documentation. Much of Micah 5:2-5 is woven into it. But Luke's primary fascination is with the fact that because of an action of the Roman government, Jesus was born in Bethlehem, fulfilling ancient prophecy. God was working his purpose out not only through the hesitancy of Zechariah, the joy of Elizabeth, and the quiet faith of Mary, but also through Caesar Augustus who, like Cyrus of old (Isa. 45:1), was God's unwitting confederate. And other symbolism also crowds to be recognized. The fact that there was no room in the inn seems to foretell the Son of man who had no place to lay his head, and ultimately no throne but a cross. Also the shepherds, those first worshipers, were forerunners of the humble multitude, who later crowded about him, and who were despised by the religious authorities because they did not, indeed could not, keep the Law with all of its intricacies. Note also the jubilation of the angelic chorus through which joy rings throughout the Gospel; it is a foretaste of the joy in heaven over penitent sinners.

2:1-20

In those days a decree went out from Caesar Augustus that all the world should be enrolled. 2 This was the first enrollment, when Quirinius was governor of Syria. 3 And all went to be enrolled, each to his own city. 4 And Joseph also went up from Galilee, from the city of Nazareth, to Judea, to the city of David, which is called Bethlehem, because he was of the house and lineage of David, 5 to be enrolled with Mary, his betrothed, who was with child. 6 And while they were there, the time came for her to be delivered. 7 And she gave birth to her first-born son and wrapped him in swaddling cloths, and laid him in a manger, because there was no place for them in the inn.

8 And in that region there were shepherds out in the field, keeping watch over their flock by night. 9 And an angel of the Lord appeared to them, and the glory of the Lord shone around them, and they were filled with fear. 10 And the angel said to them, "Be not afraid; for behold, I bring you good news of great joy which will come to all the people; 11 for to you is born this day in the city of David a Savior, who is Christ the Lord. 12 And this will be a sign for you: you will find a babe wrapped in swaddling cloths and lying in a manger." 13 And suddenly there was with the angel a multitude of the heavenly host praising God and saying,

14 "Glory to God in the highest,
   and on earth peace among men with whom he is
   pleased!"

15 When the angels went away from them into heaven, the shepherds said to one another, "Let us go over to Bethlehem and see this thing that has happened, which the Lord has made known to us." 16 And they went with haste, and found Mary and Joseph, and the babe lying in a manger. 17 And when they saw it they made known the saying which had been told them concerning this child; 18 and all who heard it wondered at what the shepherds told them. 19 But Mary kept all these things, pondering them in her heart. 20 And the shepherds returned, glorifying and praising God for all they had heard and seen, as it had been told them.

Whatever the documentary roots of the nativity stories their present literary form is due to Luke's artistic genius. Notice that while the birth of John and the birth of Jesus are placed side by side, there is no rivalry, each has his proper place and Jesus obviously has the superior place. John's birth, for instance, was greeted by prophecy from the child's father; Jesus' birth was accompanied by an angelic pronouncement of the significance of the new-born child.

The Annunciation and birth stories were probably at one time separate for Mary appears to be ignorant of any previous angelic announcement regarding the destiny of her child (2:19, also 2:33, 50-51). However, the stories were probably linked to the rest of the narrative before the document came into Luke's hands.

The Boy Jesus

The child Jesus is raised in a devout home. Indications of this are evident; he was circumcised on the eighth day, Mary's purification followed "according to the law of Moses," and his *Bar Mitzvah* took place when he reached the age of twelve. Because they live near Jerusalem Mary goes to the Temple for the Rite of Purification and there both Simeon, an ancient priest, and Anna, a venerable member of the order of widows, recognize Jesus as the Messiah. Simeon's hymn, the familiar *Nunc dimittis*, blesses God for this privileged encounter, and contains the first hint of the Messiah's universal significance:

> A light for revelation to the Gentiles,
> And for the glory of thy people Israel.

These words echo the prophetic messianic words in Isaiah 49:6. The Lord's mission will be first to the Jews and then to peoples of the whole earth. Simeon's prophecy to Mary is the first intimation of the great theme which will run throughout the Gospel: the messiah who will lead Israel to her glory will do so by treading the path of suffering.

To illustrate Jesus' thirty years of growth Luke gives one incident — the twelve-year-old boy has his *Bar Mitzvah*, becomes "a son of the Law," able to accept the responsibilities and obligations to which his parents have committed him by the rite of circumcision. An evident influence of his religious home life is that Jesus is schooled in the Scriptures during those early formative years. We can also see a developing awareness of his divine sonship. He speaks of being "in my Father's house." Henceforth, he

will not merely live under the Law but under the higher authority
of his filial consciousness.

2:21–36a

21 And at the end of eight days, when he was circumcised, he was called Jesus, the name given by the angel
before he was conceived in the womb.

22 And when the time came for their purification
according to the law of Moses, they brought him up to
Jerusalem to present him to the Lord 23 (as it is written
in the law of the Lord, "Every male that opens the
womb shall be called holy to the Lord") 24 and to offer
a sacrifice according to what is said in the law of the
Lord, "a pair of turtledoves, or two young pigeons." 25
Now there was a man in Jerusalem, whose name was
Simeon, and this man was righteous and devout, looking for the consolation of Israel, and the Holy Spirit was
upon him. 26 And it had been revealed to him by the
Holy Spirit that he should not see death before he had
seen the Lord's Christ. 27 And inspired by the Spirit he
came into the temple; and when the parents brought in
the child Jesus, to do for him according to the custom of
the law, 28 he took him up in his arms and blessed God
and said,

29 "Lord, now lettest thou thy servant, depart in
peace,
according to thy word;
30 for mine eyes have seen thy salvation
31 which thou hast prepared in the presence of all
peoples,
32 a light for revelation to the Gentiles,
and for glory to thy people Israel."

33 And his father and his mother marveled at what
was said about him; 34 and Simeon blessed them and
said to Mary his mother,

"Behold, this child is set for the fall and rising of
    many in Israel,
and for a sign that is spoken against
35 (and a sword will pierce through your own soul
also),
    that thoughts out of many hearts may be
revealed."
36 And there was a prophetess, Anna, the daughter
of Phanuel, of the tribe of Asher . . . .

2:38–52

38 And coming up at that very hour she gave thanks to
God, and spoke of him to all who were looking for the
redemption of Jerusalem.

39 And when they had performed everything according to the law of the Lord, they returned to Galilee, to
their own city, Nazareth. 40 And the child grew and
became strong, filled with wisdom; and the favor of
God was upon him.

41 Now his parents went to Jerusalem every year at
the feast of the Passover. 42 And when he was twelve
years old, they went up according to custom; 43 and
when the feast was ended, as they were returning, the
boy Jesus stayed behind in Jerusalem. His parents did
not know it, 44 but supposing him to be in the company
they went a day's journey, and they sought him among
their kinsfolk and acquaintances; 45 and when they did
not find him, they returned to Jerusalem, seeking him.
46 After three days they found him in the temple, sitting among the teachers, listening to them and asking
them questions; 47 and all who heard him were amazed
at his understanding and his answers. 48 And when
they saw him they were astonished; and his mother said
to him, "Son, why have you treated us so? Behold, your
father and I have been looking for you anxiously."

49 And he said to them, "How is it that you sought me? Did you not know that I must be in my Father's house?" 50 And they did not understand the saying which he spoke to them. 51 And he went down with them and came to Nazareth, and was obedient to them; and his mother kept all these things in her heart.

52 And Jesus increased in wisdom and in stature, and in favor with God and man.

A word about Joseph whom we meet here for the last time: he is portrayed as a law-abiding citizen, perhaps in deliberate contrast to the Zealots and other rebels against Rome. He dutifully responded to the imperial edict and took his pregnant wife to Bethlehem. And, as we have seen, Joseph and Mary raised their son in a devout home. Luke only refers to Joseph twice more and only then as part of Jesus' identity (3:23 and 4:22).

Luke has a way of using an incident as a transition piece from one part of his story to the next. The boy Jesus in the Temple is such a transition. The second section—the inauguration of his ministry—really begins here. It opens with Jesus' witness in the Temple and closes with his witness in the synagogue in Nazareth (4:16b). All that has gone before epitomized the Old Testament expectation, and Israel's yearning for the coming of the Messiah. Zechariah and Elizabeth, Joseph and Mary, Simeon and Anna are all Old Testament persons like their predecessors through the centuries, but with a difference. With them comes the beginning of the new age: they see their expectations beginning to be realized.

We turn the page to discover what that fulfillment means.

CHAPTER 3

THE SECOND BEGINNING PREPARATION FOR MINISTRY

L uke now appears to begin his account all over again with an elaborate date. Scholars disagree as to whether the birth narratives were Luke's intended beginning or whether Luke had composed a first draft before coming upon the nativity materials which he ingeniously added as a prologue. At any rate, he now settles into his account of the drama of redemption. It is eighteen years later and John is conducting a ministry of preaching and baptizing on the banks of the Jordan River. The author carefully dates the occasion—"the fifteenth year of the reign of Tiberius Caesar." He did not need any fuller date, but he goes on to identify the time with the political and religious figures of the day. He is saying that the drama of redemption is a part of world history.

John the Baptist and Jesus

The curtain rises on this drama when John the Baptist begins his ministry on the banks of the Jordan. Simeon had sung of the univeral significance of the Messiah's coming when the baby Jesus was brought to the Temple (2:32). Now Luke is going to tell what happens to Jesus the Messiah during his lifetime, and (in the Book of Acts) just how the Christian Church is involved with the Messiah's mission to the world. Indeed, when we look at Luke's carefully-planned two volumes we understand how the Christian Church comes to be the Messiah's agent through which "all flesh shall see the salvation of God" (3:6). Such is Luke's master plan.

It begins unimpressively: a man who is apparently a desert rat is preaching vociferously to a bunch of people on a river bank.

John the Baptist stands on the dividing line between the old and the new epoch. This is seen clearly in his preaching — sheer judgment, condemnation of evil. John announces the coming of the Messiah, but he cannot conceive of greatness except in terms of severity excelling his own. Wrong will be overthrown and accounts settled on a basis of strict justice. He urges the need for repentance of which the act of baptism is a symbol, but there is little mention of forgiveness (see Acts 19:4), and no good news of the Kingdom of God. (The term "good news" in vs. 18 simply means "preaching.")

Among his hearers were social outcasts who were fascinated by John. These were ordinary, selfish folk, blind to the needs of others. There were also grafting politicians and their soldier-police who expressed serious concern. But the religious leaders, who had really come to check out why this upstart was attracting such crowds, did not respond.

After John's spectacular Jordan-bank ministry Luke has him leave the stage. His ministry ends abruptly: "Herod shut up John in prison" (3:20). (We later learn of his death almost incidentally, 9:9.) The forerunner has done his job. Now attention focuses on Jesus.

He comes to be baptized by John and the new epoch dawns. Jesus' ministry will begin shortly in Galilee (4:14) but it is already quite clear that John is gone and Jesus from now on has the stage. In baptizing Jesus, John is the occasion for the inauguration of Jesus' ministry. The significance of that occasion is two-fold. Jesus comes to lead people into God's kingdom. In order to do this he must enter the kingdom by the only door open to them; that is why Jesus is baptized. He must identify with the people he came to save. He must be their representative before he can be their king. "He was numbered with the transgressors," had been the prophet's insight long ago (Isa. 53:12). The other significant aspect of the occasion is that "the Holy Spirit descended upon him."

"When Jesus also had been baptized and was praying, the heaven was opened." The event is a vision of pivotal importance. Jesus is the one who is imbued with the Spirit. This real possession of the Holy Spirit is basic to Luke's whole understanding of the ministry of Jesus; he is the one through whom God acts. The words of the heavenly voice are from texts used in Judaism to describe the Messiah (Ps. 2:7 and Isa. 42:1). Psalm 2 proclaims the ascension of the king who is to rule with a rod of iron; and Isaiah 42:1-6, the first of the Servant poems, describes the Servant of the Lord who is chosen to carry true religion to the Gentiles and who, in achieving that mission, must suffer indignity, rejection, and death. Jesus, "my well-beloved Son," now knows that he not only stands in a special relationship with God, but he also knows what that entails.

The point of the genealogy which follows is to lay to rest any thought that if Jesus was Son of God then he was only partly human. Luke makes clear that he is bound by ties of blood not only to Israel right on back to Abraham, but to all of humanity. He is "the son of Adam, the son of God." The mission of this son of Adam will be to all sons and daughters of Adam, not just to the children of Abraham.

3:1-23, 34, 38

> In the fifteenth year of the reign of Tiberius Caesar, Pontius Pilate being governor of Judea, and Herod being tetrarch of Galilee, and his brother Philip tetrarch of the region of Ituraea and Trachonitis and Lysanias tetrarch of Abilene, 2 in the high-priesthood of Annas and Caiaphas, the word of God came to John the son of Zechariah in the wilderness; 3 and he went into all the region about the Jordan, preaching a baptism of repentance for the forgiveness of sin. 4 As it is written in the book of the words of Isaiah the prophet,
> "The voice of one crying in the wilderness:
> Prepare the way of the Lord,

make his paths straight.
5 Every valley shall be filled,
and every mountain and hill shall be brought low,
and the crooked shall be made straight,
and the rough ways shall be made smooth;
6 and all flesh shall see the salvation of God."

7 He said therefore to the multitudes that came out to be baptized by him, "You brood of vipers! Who warned you to flee from the wrath to come? 8 Bear fruits that befit repentance, and do not begin to say to yourselves, 'We have Abraham as our father'; for I tell you, God is able from these stones to raise up children to Abraham. 9 Even now the ax is laid to the root of the trees; every tree therefore that does not bear good fruit is cut down and thrown into the fire."

10 And the multitudes asked him, "What then shall we do?" 11 And he answered them, "He who has two coats, let him share with him who has none; and he who has food, let him do likewise." 12 Tax collectors also came to be baptized, and said to him, "Teacher, what shall we do?" 13 And he said to them, "Collect no more than is appointed you." 14 Soldiers also asked him, "And we, what shall we do?" And he said to them, "Rob no one by violence or by false accusation, and be content with your wages."

15 As the people were in expectation, and all men questioned in their hearts concerning John, whether perhaps he were the Christ, 16 John answered them all, "I baptize you with water; but he who is mightier than I is coming, the thong of whose sandals I am not worthy to untie; he will baptize you with the Holy Spirit and with fire. 17 His winnowing fork is in his hand, to clear his threshing floor, and to gather the wheat into his granary, but the chaff he will burn with unquenchable fire."

18 So, with many other exhortations, he preached

good news to the people. 19 But Herod the tetrarch, who had been reproved by him for Herodias, his brother's wife, and for all the evil things that Herod had done, 20 added this to them all, that he shut up John in prison.

21 Now when all the people were baptized, and when Jesus also had been baptized and was praying, the heaven was opened, 22 and the Holy Spirit descended upon him in bodily form, as a dove, and a voice came from heaven, "Thou art my beloved Son; with thee I am well pleased."

23 Jesus, when he began his ministry, was about thirty years of age, being the son (as was supposed) of Joseph, the son of Heli . . . the son of Abraham . . . the son of Adam, the son of God.

Jesus was praying when the heavenly voice and the gift of the Holy Spirit came to him. Throughout the Gospel Luke continually pictures Jesus as a man of prayer (5:16; 6:12; 9:18 and 28; 11:1; 22:41; 23:34). And he commends this way of life to those around him: people "ought always to pray and not lose heart" (18:1). It is not surprising that in the resurrection appearance to the disciples in Emmaus they recognized him when he was praying (24:30-31) — that was so characteristic of him.

The Temptations in the Wilderness

Since his baptism in the Jordan, Jesus is the sole bearer of the Holy Spirit which now leads him into the wilderness where he is tempted by the devil. Notice the nature of his temptation. The attractive, strongest temptations concern what appears to be good. Jesus' temptations are presented as ways to prove his messiahship and to double check on the reality of his heavenly vision. Here are opportunities to demonstrate his messiahship and to win people and kingdoms. Why not turn stones into bread? To a people accustomed to privation the heavenly banquet of the messianic age was longed for (Isa. 25:6-8). Again: he wanted to have the kingdoms of the world recognize his lordship. How easy to bow the knee to the devil for one brief moment and win that prize. And finally: he relies on the Heavenly Father's care and protection. Why not make it evident by a spectacular leap into the arms of the guardian angels? The devil pictures messiahship as an opportunity for self-aggrandizement and self-glory. But Jesus counters him with his scriptual awareness of the true nature of his mission. He makes it clear that proper desires fulfilled in an improper context become sinful.

4:1-13

> And Jesus, full of the Holy Spirit, returned from the Jordan, and was led by the Spirit 2 for forty days in the wilderness, tempted by the devil. And he ate nothing in those days; and when they were ended, he was hungry. 3 The devil said to him, "If you are the Son of God, command this stone to become bread." 4 And Jesus answered him, "It is written, 'Man shall not live by bread alone.'" 5 And the devil took him up, and showed him all the kingdoms of the world in a moment of time, 6 and said to him, "To you I will give all this authority and their glory; for it has been delivered to me, and I give it to whom I will. 7 If you, then, will worship me, it shall all be yours." 8 And Jesus answered him, "It is written,
>
> > 'You shall worship the Lord your God,
> > and him only shall you serve.'"
>
> 9 And he took him to Jerusalem, and set him on the pinnacle of the temple, and said to him, "If you are the Son of God, throw yourself down from here; 10 for it is written,
>
> > 'He will give his angels charge of you, to guard you, 11 and
> >
> > 'On their hands they will bear you up,
> > lest you strike your foot against a stone.'"

12 And Jesus answered him, "It is said, 'You shall not tempt the Lord your God.'" 13 And when the devil had ended every temptation, he departed from him until an opportune time.

In these temptations Jesus is not attacked at a point of weakness but rather at the point of his greatest strength—his compassion, his commitment, his faith. Such are the wiles of the devil. In each case Jesus puts himself under the authority of Scripture and so under the authority of God.

Luke's Gospel is full of symbolism. Notice that for the second temptation the devil simply "took him up and showed him all the kingdoms of the world." There is no mention of a mountain as in Matthew (Mt. 4:8). A mountain has symbolic significance for Luke; it is a place of prayer and meditation, not a location for temptation or for public preaching. See how this symbolism runs through the whole Gospel. After a night of prayer in the hills, Jesus chooses his twelve disciples; then "he came down with them and stood on a level place" to deliver Luke's counterpart of the Sermon on the Mount (6:12, 17). Later, the Transfiguration takes place on a mountain (9:28). And, of course, he was praying on the Mount of Olives prior to his final arrest (22:39).

The Temple also holds a place of importance in the pattern of Luke's Gospel. It is not accidental that the last temptation takes place at the Temple. Luke characteristically ends blocks of material at the Temple—the birth-infant narratives (2:46), the end of Jesus' public ministry (21:37), the end of the Gospel (24:53), all are in the Temple. Luke's is the most churchy of the four Gospels.

"When the devil had ended every temptation"—this seems to suggest that there were more than three temptations, and that the recorded ones are perhaps representative. They show the nature of temptation and of Jesus' reaction. Notice also that temptation is not permanently ended—the devil "departed until an opportune time." He does not appear again until he enters Judas (22:3). Jesus' life is a time when the devil has been expelled, a time when God's purposes are being fulfilled in history. That

Jesus is truly Son of God is proven by his defeat of the devil and his repeated victories over demonic powers (10:18; 11:14-18; 13:16). We will hear the voice of temptation on one later occasion. It will sound almost like an echo blown by the wind across the years from his wilderness experience: "He saved others; let him save himself, if he is the Christ of God, his Chosen One!" (22:35). It will be Satan's final effort to corrupt the Son of God as he hangs on the cross.

In the Nazareth Synagogue

In the temptations Jesus' endowment with the Spirit is made manifest and Satan has to yield. In what follows we see the redemptive character of a period free from Satan. The Spirit now leads Jesus into Galilee. Luke begins the account of Jesus' ministry with the synagogue experience in Nazareth as a transition piece.

Luke has selected this incident from material about the Galilean mininstry because it will best set the stage for an understanding of the events that follow. The people in Jesus' hometown had heard about his ministry in other parts of Galilee. So when he attended the synagogue in Nazareth Jesus was invited to take part, to read the Scripture and comment on it. He reads an Isaiah passage which is obviously about the Messiah. The neighbors hear him with enthusiasm, but when they realize that he has laid claim to the passage — it is not about someone who is to come, but about himself — admiration turns to doubt. They want some proof of his preposterous claim so that they can decide whether they think he is the Messiah. But to Jesus the desire for a sign is satanic. Signs are not for skeptics, but for believers. ("Your faith has made you whole," he was to say more than once in the days ahead.) The congregation's mood changes as quickly as a chameleon on a patchwork quilt — from doubt to hostility to angry violence. For Jesus has reminded them through stories of Elijah and Elisha that God's compassionate concern for people ignores class and race, and is only limited by the faith to receive it. They recognize this as a judgment on their smugness and the congregation becomes a lynch mob.

Jesus is put out of the city (a foreshadowing of the crucifixion; executions were not done within the walls) and would have been killed. However, his hour has not yet come and he is divinely protected from harm. His escape makes possible a mission elsewhere, just as his resurrection will make possible a mission to the world.

4:14–30

14 And Jesus returned in the power of the Spirit into Galilee, and a report concerning him went out through all the surrounding country. 15 And he taught in their synagogues, being glorified by all.

16 And he came to Nazareth, where he had been brought up; and he went to the synagogue, as his custom was, on the sabbath day. And he stood up to read; 17 and there was given to him the book of the prophet Isaiah. He opened the book, and found the place where it was written,

18 "The Spirit of the Lord is upon me,

because he has anointed me to preach good news to the poor.

He has sent me to proclaim release to the captives and recovering of sight to the blind,

to set at liberty those who are oppressed,

19 to proclaim the acceptable year of the Lord."

20 And he closed the book, and gave it back to the attendant, and sat down; and the eyes of all the synagogue were fixed on him. 21 And he began to say to them, "Today this scripture has been fulfilled in your hearing." 22 And all spoke well of him, and wondered at the gracious words which proceeded out of his mouth; and they said, "Is not this Joseph's son?" 23 And he said to them, "Doubtless you will quote to me this proverb, 'Physician, heal yourself; what we have heard you did

at Capernaum, do here also in your own country.'" 24 And he said, "Truly, I say to you, no prophet is acceptable in his own country. 25 But in truth, I tell you, there were many widows in Israel in the days of Elijah, when the heaven was shut up three years and six months, when there came a great famine over all the land; 26 and Elijah was sent to none of them but only to Zarephath, in the land of Sidon, to a woman who was a widow. 27 And there were many lepers in Israel in the time of the prophet Elisha; and none of them was cleansed, but only Naaman the Syrian." 28 When they heard this, all in the synagogue were filled with wrath. 29 And they rose up and put him out of the city, and led him to the brow of the hill on which their city was built, that they might throw him down headlong. 30 But passing through the midst of them he went away.

Two points stand out in Luke's first recorded incident of Jesus' public ministry. First, while it is not surprising that Jesus claims to be the bearer of the Holy Spirit (as the Isaiah reading makes clear), it is surprising that he sees his messiahship involved in bringing salvation to the Gentiles. This emphasis is seen here in his Elijah and Elisha illustrations, and will be seen repeatedly in other teachings and actions, for Jesus goes out of his way to show an interest in and concern for non-Jews. The mission is first to the Jews (most of whom refuse it) and then to the Gentiles. This is one of Luke's recurring themes. Jesus' all-embracing view of his messiahship starts here like the beginning ripples caused when a pebble is thrown into a pool. Before Luke lays down his pen, those ripples of salvation will extend from Jerusalem and all Judea to Samaria and on to the ends of the earth (Acts 1:8).

CHAPTER 4

THE GALILEAN MINISTRY

Nazareth is in the hill country 1300 feet above the Sea of Galilee. Jesus goes down to Capernaum, a trading center on the shore of that sea, which becomes the hub of his Galilean ministry. He regularly attends the synagogue and they welcome him as a preacher for there is an authoritative freshness in his words. People recognize that here is a man with intimate knowledge of God. That first Sabbath day in the synagogue he heals a demon-possessed man. In those times demon possession included any ailment which caused one to lose control — epilepsy, convulsions, nervous disorder, etc. — for it suggested that an evil power had taken hold of the individual. Modern medicine would describe such afflictions otherwise; actually, that first century designation was primarily a religious description. The kingdom of evil has extended its rule into a person's life from which he can be rescued only by the superior power of God. Jesus is the warrior of the kingdom of God doing battle with those nefarious forces which seek to limit the area of God's kingly reign and authority. Every cure is a victory in the spiritual battle between the Christ (the Messiah), agent of the kingdom of God, and the forces of the kingdom of evil. Every healing, therefore, is a dramatic proclamation of the good news of the arrival of the kingdom of God.

4:31–44

> 31 And he went down to Capernaum, a city of Galilee. And he was teaching them on the sabbath; 32 and

they were astonished at his teaching, for his word was with authority. 33 And in the synagogue there was a man who had the spirit of an unclean demon; and he cried out with a loud voice, 34 "Ah! What have you to do with us, Jesus of Nazareth? Have you come to destroy us? I know who you are, the Holy One of God." 35 But Jesus rebuked him, saying, "Be silent, and come out of him!" And when the demon had thrown him down in the midst, he came out of him, having done him no harm. 36 And they were all amazed and said to one another, "What is this word? For with authority and power he commands the unclean spirits, and they come out." 37 And reports of him went out into every place in the surrounding region.

38 And he arose and left the synagogue, and entered Simon's house. Now Simon's mother-in-law was ill with a high fever, and they besought him for her. 39 And he stood over her and rebuked the fever, and it left her; and immediately she rose and served them.

40 Now when the sun was setting, all those who had any that were sick with various diseases brought them to him; and he laid his hands on every one of them and healed them. 41 And demons also came out of many, crying, "You are the Son of God!" But he rebuked them, and would not allow them to speak, because they knew that he was the Christ.

42 And when it was day he departed and went into a lonely place. And the people sought him and came to him, and would have kept him from leaving them; 43 but he said to them, "I must preach the good news of the kingdom of God to the other cities also; for I was sent for this purpose." 44 And he was preaching in the synagogues of Judea.

The kingdom of God is the main theme of Jesus' teaching. Here we have the first mention of it at the end of that busy Sabbath day in Capernaum. The term kingdom of God means that God is the eternal King who has a purpose for history, and Israel is the agent for fulfilling that purpose. The Jews looked forward longingly to the day when God would openly show his power and assume the authority which was rightfully his. Now Jesus who is the Christ (which is the Greek translation of the Hebrew title *messiah*, meaning "anointed") is doing just that. The Christ is God's appointed representative who is to be the Savior of all humanity. Because of him, people receive salvation in "the forgiveness of their sins, through the tender mercy of our God" (1:77-78). But he does not want his identity disclosed (by the demons or anyone else), because he consistently refuses to be identified publicly as "Messiah" since the term is so easily misconstrued. It had political and nationalistic overtones which were not part of his mission.

"Follow Me"

Jesus now begins to gather about him an inner circle of disciples. The call to be a disciple of a rabbi was serious business. When a rabbi or teacher said to a young man, "Follow me," what he meant was, "Leave your family and your business and your home and your possessions and become one of my special pupils." If a man accepted this invitation, he left all his former life behind and lived wherever his rabbi lived. He followed his rabbi obediently and saw that all the rabbi's needs were met. A disciple had to do all the things a personal slave would be expected to do except to stoop down and untie his master's sandals. (When John the Baptist said that he was not worthy even to untie the sandals of the Coming One, he meant that Christ would be so much greater than he that he would not be worthy even to be his slave.)

A disciple was expected to memorize everything his rabbi taught him. This is the way learning was passed on. The rabbi spoke for a certain length of time, and then he stopped and listened to his disciples who were expected to repeat what he had said. In this way, they finally memorized the whole teaching of their rabbi. The other part of the disciples' responsibility was perhaps even more important, for by living with their teacher they learned from his example. Thus the rabbi and his disciples made a very special kind of group. A disciple remained with his rabbi until he had learned all that his rabbi could teach him; then he became a rabbi himself.

Jesus calls Simon Peter and his associates to be his disciples. Their call follows the miracle of an amazing catch of fish which is probably recorded to illustrate the Lord's authority over nature. More importantly, the incident shows Jesus' miraculous influence upon dispirited individuals.

5:1–11

> While the people pressed upon him to hear the word of God, he was standing by the lake of Gennesaret. 2 And he saw two boats by the lake; but the fishermen had gone out of them and were washing their nets. 3 Getting into one of the boats, which was Simon's, he asked him to put out a little from the land. And he sat down and taught the people from the boat. 4 And when he had ceased speaking, he said to Simon, "Put out into the deep and let down your nets for a catch." 5 And Simon answered, "Master, we toiled all night and took nothing! But at your word I will let down the nets." 6 And when they had done this, they enclosed a great shoal of fish; and as their nets were breaking, 7 they beckoned to their partners in the other boat to come and help them. And they came and filled both the boats, so that they began to sink. 8 But when Simon Peter saw it, he fell down at Jesus' knees, saying, "Depart from me, for I am a sinful man, O Lord." 9 For he was astonished, and all that were with him, at the catch of fish which they had taken; 10 and so also were James and John, sons of Zebedee, who were partners with Simon. And Jesus said to Simon, "Do not be

> afraid; henceforth you will be catching men." 11 And
> when they had brought their boats to land, they left
> everything and followed him.

The abiding significance of this incident is that what the Lord commands, he empowers one to perform. Peter and his friends had "toiled all night and caught nothing." But when they obeyed Jesus' command, their nets were full. Peter knows himself to be a sinful, inadequate person but, even so, in accepting the Lord's invitation to follow him, he is promised that he "will be catching men."

"*They* left everything and followed him." The story is based in part on Mark 1:16-20 from which we gather that there were four of them — "Simon and Andrew the brother of Simon," and "James the son of Zebedee and John his brother." This incident is probably told in order to accent the primary importance of Simon Peter's role among Jesus' disciples.

The place of miracles in Luke's Gospel is worth noting. He sets miracles above preaching. In Matthew it is the other way around. It is not until after the Sermon on the Mount that Matthew reports any miracles. While this incident in Luke also begins with a sermon, it does not contain any teaching; rather it indicates that one of the results of miracles will be the rejection of Jesus (4:23-28). And here we see that the actual event of choosing disciples is immediately linked with a miracle. Luke's order, then, is miracle, discipleship, then teaching, a sequence which John's Gospel is also inclined to follow (John 9:1-38).

Healing a Leper

Jesus' popularity is growing. We saw early evidence of this in the way the people of Capernaum received him (4:40, 42-43). Now when he heals a poor leper it becomes more widespread — "great multitudes gather to hear and to be healed of their infirmities." This occasion is the first evidence that through the power of the Spirit Jesus is bringing "release to the captives"(4:18).

5:12-16

12 While he was in one of the cities, there came a man full of leprosy; and when he saw Jesus, he fell on his face and besought him, "Lord, if you will, you can make me clean." 13 And he stretched out his hand, and touched him, saying, "I will; be clean." And immediately the leprosy left him. 14 And he charged him to tell no one; but "go and show yourself to the priest, and make an offering for your cleansing, as Moses commanded, for a proof to the people." 15 But so much the more the report went abroad concerning him; and great multitudes gathered to hear and to be healed of their infirmities. 16 But he withdrew to the wilderness and prayed.

The sympathy and compassion of the Lord is nowhere better described than in the words, "he touched him." Lepers were outcasts. They were required to stay yards away from a public road and to call out, "Unclean, unclean," to warn passersby of their presence. Their suffering was not only physical, it was also social and emotional — they longed for human companionship and warmth. By his touch Jesus breaks down that cruel social barrier. By healing him Jesus restores that outcast to society. No wonder word spread and people flocked to him.

Every time Jesus' life becomes too crowded and demanding, he withdraws to some quiet place and prays. We saw him do this after the busy Sabbath day in Capernaum (4:42-43), and here again he withdraws "to the wilderness and prays." It is the habit of "the beloved Son in whom I am well pleased" to keep in continual touch with the Father whose will he had come to do on earth.

Opposition Begins to Build

The crescendo of public acclaim brought Jesus to the attention of the religious authorities. The Jewish leaders in Jerusalem had a working relationship with their Roman oppressors. As long as taxes were paid the High Priest and the Sanhedrin, the supreme court in Jewish theocracy, had a relatively free hand in conducting the affairs of the nation. So they were watchful of and sensitive to any movement which might disturb public peace and give the Romans an excuse to take over in a heavy-handed way. They had kept a nervous eye on John the Baptist until Herod had removed him from the scene. Now here is Jesus—a disciple of John, perhaps? He had been baptized in the Jordan and he is attracting large crowds. He must be watched. The Pharisees and their scribes who taught the Law were the authorities who saw to it that God's Law was properly respected and observed. These observers watch Jesus, and no doubt report to the authorities in Jerusalem.

5:17–28

17 On one of those days, as he was teaching, there were Pharisees and teachers of the law sitting by, who had come from every village of Galilee and Judea and from Jerusalem; and the power of the Lord was with him to heal. 18 And behold, men were bringing on a bed a man who was paralyzed, and they sought to bring him in and lay him before Jesus; 19 but finding no way to bring him in, because of the crowd, they went up on the roof and let him down with his bed through the tiles into the midst before Jesus. 20 And when he saw their faith he said, "Man, your sins are forgiven you." 21 And the scribes and the Pharisees began to question, saying, "Who is this that speaks blasphemies? Who can forgive sins but God only?" 22 When Jesus perceived their questioning, he answered them, "Why do you question in your hearts? 23 Which is easier, to say, 'Your sins are forgiven you,' or to say, 'Rise and walk'? 24 But that you may know that the Son of man has authority on earth to forgive sins" — he said to the man who was paralyzed — "I say to you, rise, take up your bed and go home."

25 And immediately he rose before them, and took up that on which he lay, and went home, glorifying God. 26 And amazement seized them all, and they glorified God and were filled with awe, saying, "We have seen strange things today." 27 After this he went out, and saw a tax collector, named Levi, sitting at the tax office; and he said to him, "Follow me." 28 And he left everything, and rose and followed him.

6:1–11

On a sabbath, while he was going through the grainfields, his disciples plucked and ate some ears of grain, rubbing them in their hands. 2 But some of the Pharisees said, "Why are you doing what is not lawful to do on the sabbath?" 3 And Jesus answered, "Have you not read what David did when he was hungry, he and those who were with him: 4 how he entered the house of God, and took and ate the bread of the Presence, which it is not lawful for any but the priests to eat, and also gave it to those with him?" 5 And he said to them, "The Son of man is lord of the sabbath."

6 On another sabbath, when he entered the synagogue and taught, a man was there whose right hand was withered. 7 And the scribes and the Pharisees watched him, to see whether he would heal on the sabbath, so that they might find an accusation against him. 8 But he knew their thoughts, and he said to the man who had the withered hand, "Come and stand here." And he rose and stood there. 9 And Jesus said to them, "I ask you, is it lawful on the sabbath to do good or to do harm, to save life or to destroy it?" 10 And he looked around on them all, and said to him, "Stretch out your hand." And he did so, and his hand was restored. 11 But they were filled with fury and discussed with one another what they might do to Jesus.

To these Pharisee observers Jesus is dangerous. If he has his way, they think, the duty of keeping the Law will be ignored. The whole religious outlook will be changed. Look what he is doing! First, in the course of his teaching (probably in the synagogue) he offers forgiveness to a paralyzed man before the fellow has earned it. Such a thing is blasphemy, for it belittles God's way of forgiving. God's forgiveness is not freely given to anyone who might want it. One has to work for it. Anyone who misleads people in this way is dangerous. Such a person must be stopped.

Second, Jesus associates with the wrong people. No righteous man would mix with "sinners," at least not until they changed their ways. Jesus even includes tax collectors in his company. (The Jews who collected the Roman taxes were classed with 'sinners' for two reasons: first, they were often dishonest grafters who charged people more than they owed; second, because of their dealing with Gentiles, they were 'unclean.') No righteous man associates with tax collectors, but Jesus does. Of course, the Pharisees want sinners to repent, but until they do, the Pharisees have nothing to do with them. The high standards of the Law must be upheld. So Jesus is setting a very bad example. He must be stopped.

For many of the Pharisees, keeping the Sabbath Day holy was the most important law of all. In order to do this they carefully avoided any suggestion of work which might break the law. They are upset at Jesus, for while he and his disciples are walking through a grain field on the Sabbath they rub the outer husks from kernels of grain between the palms of their hands and eat the grain. "Work!" said the Pharisees. "Threshing grain is work, no matter how small the amount."

The Pharisees become even more upset when, in answer to their criticism, Jesus explains the observance of the Sabbath in a new way. And he goes on to say, "The Son of man is lord of the Sabbath." Jesus is assuming blasphemous authority, and, in their eyes, destroying the Law.

Now Jesus has some real enemies. The Pharisees, good and respectable as they are, see Jesus as one who is pulling to pieces the precious practices and laws and customs which the Jews had accepted for hundreds of years. They are concerned and, no doubt, when the report reaches Jerusalem, the religious authorities there are equally concerned. They begin to plot how they can destroy him.

Inaugurating the New Israel

In the face of the growing hostility of the Pharisees Jesus must now decide what to do. Characteristically, he faces the decision in a night of prayer, and it is, not surprisingly, in the hills — the place of meditation and revelation. With the coming of day he has his decision and he takes resolute action. He chooses twelve apostles from the ranks of his faithful disciples; that is, he reconstitutes the twelve-tribe framework of the people of God — the New Israel. Luke prematurely calls them "apostles," a word not applied to The Twelve as a technical term until near the end of the first century (Rev. 21:14). We know something definite about only three or four of these most ordinary men; even the names of the others are uncertain. Legend and imagination have supplied posterity with details about them.

Then, accompanied by the The Twelve, Jesus goes down to "a level place" where he meets the larger circle of his disciples. They are not only "from all Judea and Jerusalem" but even from Tyre and Sidon, seacoast towns several days journey to the north and west. Jesus' fame has spread, and these have come to hear him and to be healed of their diseases. This sermon is a sort of inaugural address to the New Israel, setting forth the promises and principles of the new age, the impending kingdom of God.

6:12–49

12 In these days he went out to the mountain to pray; and all night he continued in prayer to God. 13 And when it was day, he called his disciples, and chose from them twelve, whom he named apostles; 14 Simon, whom

he named Peter, and Andrew his brother, and James and John, and Philip, and Bartholomew, 15 and Matthew, and Thomas, and James the son of Alphaeus, and Simon who was called the Zealot, 16 and Judas the son of James, and Judas Iscariot, who became a traitor.

17 And he came down with them and stood on a level place, with a great crowd of his disciples and a great multitude of people from all Judea and Jerusalem and the seacoast of Tyre and Sidon, who came to hear him and to be healed of their diseases; 18 and those who were troubled with unclean spirits were cured. 19 And all the crowd sought to touch him, for power came forth from him and healed them all.

20 And he lifted up his eyes on his disciples, and said:

"Blessed are you poor, for yours is the kingdom of God.

21 "Blessed are you that hunger now, for you shall be satisfied.

"Blessed are you that weep now, for you shall laugh.

22 "Blessed are you when men hate you, and when they exclude you and revile you, and cast out your name as evil on account of the Son of man! 23 Rejoice in that day, and leap for joy, for behold, your reward is great in heaven; for so their fathers did to the prophets.

24 "But woe to you that are rich, for you have received your consolation.

25 "Woe to you that are full now, for you shall hunger.

"Woe to you that laugh now, for you shall mourn and weep.

26 "Woe to you, when all men speak well of you, for so their fathers did to the false prophets.

27 "But I say to you that hear, Love your enemies, do good to those who hate you, 28 bless those who curse you, pray for those who abuse you. 29 To him who

strikes you on the cheek, offer the other also; and from him who takes away your cloak do not withhold even your shirt. 30 Give to every one who begs from you; and of him who takes away your goods, do not ask them again. 31 And as you wish that men would do to you, do so to them.

32 "If you love those who love you, what credit is that to you? For even sinners love those who love them. 33 And if you do good to those who do good to you, what credit is that to you? For even sinners do the same. 34 And if you lend to those from whom you hope to receive, what credit is that to you? Even sinners lend to sinners, to receive as much again. 35 But love your enemies, and do good, and lend, expecting nothing in return; and your reward will be great, and you will be sons of the Most High; for he is kind to the ungrateful and the selfish. 36 Be merciful, even as your Father is merciful.

37 "Judge not, and you will not be judged; condemn not, and you will not be condemned; forgive, and you will be forgiven; 38 give, and it will be given to you; good measure, pressed down, shaken together, running over, will be put into your lap. For the measure you give will be the measure you get back."

39 He also told them a parable: "Can a blind man lead a blind man? Will they not both fall into a pit? 40 A disciple is not above his teacher, but every one when he is fully taught will be like his teacher. 41 Why do you see the speck that is in your brother's eye, but do not notice the log that is in your own eye? 42 Or how can you say to your brother, 'Brother, let me take out the speck that is in your eye,' when you yourself do not see the log that is in your own eye? You hypocrite, first take the log out of your own eye, and then you will see clearly to take out the speck that is in your brother's eye.

43 "For no good tree bears bad fruit, nor again does a

bad tree bear good fruit; 44 for each tree is known by its own fruit. For figs are not gathered from thorns, nor are grapes picked from a bramble bush. 45 The good man out of the good treasure of his heart produces good, and the evil man out of his evil treasure produces evil; for out of the abundance of the heart his mouth speaks.

46 "Why do you call me 'Lord, Lord,' and not do what I tell you? 47 Every one who comes to me and hears my words and does them, I will show you what he is like: 48 he is like a man building a house, who dug deep, and laid the foundation upon rock; and when a flood arose, the stream broke against that house, and could not shake it, because it had been well built. 49 But he who hears and does not do them is like a man who built a house on the ground without a foundation; against which the stream broke, and immediately it fell, and the ruin of that house was great."

"The Sermon on the Plain," as it is called, is similar to the Sermon on the Mount in Matthew. They both begin with beatitudes and end with the Parable of the Two Houses. Both sermons come from the "Q" source to which Matthew added some other materials.

Characteristics of the Kingdom

The four subsequent stories throw light on the characteristics of the coming kingdom. The kingdom is to be received by faith. The faith of a Roman centurion whose slave is ill and the faith of a prostitute whose sins are forgiven make this graphic (7:1-10; 36-50). With the coming of the kingdom there will be deliverance from death which is signaled by the raising of the son of the widow of Nain (7:17). And the fourth incident is the questioning of the delegation from the imprisoned John the Baptist, and Jesus' subsequent comments: John typifies the best of the old age but the new age far surpasses it (7:18-35). So the unprivileged group—the poor, the afflicted, the Gentiles, the immoral—are welcomed into the kingdom; while the satisfied, the privileged, and the "religious" reject God's redemptive purpose (7:30).

Look at two of these incidents—the delegation from John and the penitent prostitute.

7:19–30

19 And John, calling to him two of his disciples, sent them to the Lord, saying, "Are you he who is to come, or shall we look for another?" 20 And when the men had come to him, they said, "John the Baptist has sent us to you, saying, 'Are you he who is to come, or shall we look for another?'" 21 In that hour he cured many of diseases and plagues and evil spirits, and on many that were blind he bestowed sight. 22 And he answered them, "Go and tell John what you have seen and heard: the blind receive their sight, the lame walk, lepers are cleansed, and the deaf hear, the dead are raised up, the poor have good news preached to them. 23 And blessed is he who takes no offence at me!"

24 When the messengers of John had gone, he began to speak to the crowds concerning John: "What did you go out into the wilderness to behold? A reed shaken by the wind? 25 What then did you go out to see? A man clothed in soft clothing? Behold, those who are gorgeously appareled and live in luxury are in kings' courts. 26 What then did you go out to see? A prophet? Yes, I tell you, and more than a prophet. 27 This is he of whom it is written,

'Behold, I send my messenger before thy face,
who shall prepare thy way before thee.'

28 I tell you, among those born of women none is greater than John; yet he who is least in the kingdom of God is greater than he." 29 (When they heard this all

the people and the tax collectors justified God, having been baptized with the baptism of John; 30 but the Pharisees and the lawyers rejected the purpose of God for themselves, not having been baptized by him.) . . .

7:36–50

36 One of the Pharisees asked him to eat with him, and he went into the Pharisee's house, and took his place at table. 37 And behold, a woman of the city, who was a sinner, when she learned that he was at table in the Pharisee's house, brought an alabaster flask of ointment, 38 and standing behind him at his feet, weeping, she began to wet his feet with her tears, and wiped them with the hair of her head, and kissed his feet, and anointed them with the ointment. 39 Now when the Pharisee who had invited him saw it, he said to himself, "If this man were a prophet, he would have known who and what sort of woman this is who is touching him, for she is a sinner." 40 And Jesus answering said to him, "Simon, I have something to say to you." And he answered, "What is it, Teacher?" 41 "A certain creditor had two debtors; one owed five hundred denarii, and the other fifty. 42 When they could not pay, he forgave them both. Now which of them will love him more?" 43 Simon answered, "The one, I suppose, to whom he forgave more." And he said to him, "You have judged rightly." 44 Then turning toward the woman he said to Simon, "Do you see this woman? I entered your house, you gave me no water for my feet, but she has wet my feet with her tears and wiped them with her hair. 45 You gave me no kiss, but from the time I came in she has not ceased to kiss my feet. 46 You did not anoint my head with oil, but she has anointed my feet with ointment. 47 Therefore I tell you, her sins, which are many, are forgiven, for she loved much; but

he who is forgiven little, loves little." 48 And he said to her, "Your sins are forgiven." 49 Then those who were at table with him began to say among themselves, "Who is this, who even forgives sins?" 50 And he said to the woman, "Your faith has saved you; go in peace."

Luke never misses an opportunity to relate the material at hand to something which has gone before. Here the message Jesus sends back to John is essentially in the words of Isaiah which the Lord had read in the Nazareth synagogue (4:18-19). It answers John's question, "Are you he who is to come?" that is, the Messiah. The Isaiah passage is describing the deeds of the Messiah, the very deeds which Jesus is doing.

The story of that penitent woman conveys the same sympathy and compassion we have seen earlier in Jesus' dealings with the leper (5:12-16). In the case of the woman, Jesus is saying that great love can be the result of great forgiveness. Her love was not the reason for her pardon; rather, it was her response to being forgiven. That same characteristic of interacting love and forgiveness is demanded, Jesus says, of those who would enter the kingdom (6:27, 37)).

Preaching the Kingdom

The character of Jesus' ministry now changes. His ministry has previously been conducted principally in the synagogues; now it becomes a systematic visiting of towns and villages along with The Twelve. We catch a brief glimpse of the supporting circle of women, people whom he had helped and healed, who accompany them and provide for their needs. (See also 23:27 and Mark 15:40-41.) The accent has shifted from Christ's person to his mission — "preaching and bringing the good news of the kingdom of God."

There is an emphasis throughout on the fact that there will be overwhelming rejection, but where there is faith the good news of the kingdom will be evident. This is first set forth in the Parable of the Sower, more properly the Parable of the Seed and the Soils. Of the four types of soil—the hardened, the superficial, the double-minded, and the right hearers—only the last produces the fruit of witnessing and obedience.

With the coming of his family from Nazareth this point is graphically illustrated. The Messiah's brothers (Abraham's children, 3:8) have no priority in the kingdom of God. The true brothers and sisters of Jesus are sons and daughters to God and to be that they must do the will of their Father.

8:1–15

Soon afterward he went on through cities and villages, preaching and bringing the good news of the kingdom of God. And the twelve were with him, 2 and also some women who had been healed of evil spirits and infirmities: Mary, called Magdalene, from whom seven demons had gone out, 3 and Joanna, the wife of Chuza, Herod's steward, and Susanna, and many others, who provided for them out of their means.

4 And when a great crowd came together and people from town after town came to him, he said in a parable: 5 "A sower went out to sow his seed; and as he sowed, some fell along the path, and was trodden under foot, and the birds of the air devoured it. 6 And some fell on the rock; and as it grew up, it withered away, because it had no moisture. 7 And some fell among thorns; and the thorns grew with it and choked it. 8 And some fell into good soil and grew, and yielded a hundredfold." As he said this, he called out, "He who has ears to hear, let him hear."

9 And when his disciples asked him what this parable meant, 10 he said, "To you it has been given to know the secrets of the kingdom of God; but for others they are in parables, so that seeing they may not see, and hearing they may not understand. 11 Now the parable

is this: The seed is the word of God. 12 The ones along the path are those who have heard; then the devil comes and takes away the word from their hearts, that they may not believe and be saved. 13 And the ones on the rock are those who, when they hear the word, receive it with joy; but these have no root, they believe for a while and in time of temptation fall away. 14 And as for what fell among the thorns, they are those who hear, but as they go on their way they are choked by the cares and riches and pleasures of life, and their fruit does not mature. 15 And as for that in the good soil, they are those who, hearing the word, hold it fast in an honest and good heart, and bring forth fruit with patience...."

8:19–21

19 Then his mother and his brothers came to him, but they could not reach him for the crowd. 20 And he was told, "Your mother and your brothers are standing outside, desiring to see you." 21 But he said to them, "My mother and my brothers are those who hear the word of God and do it."

Now come two miracles—a nature miracle and a miracle of healing—which illustrate Jesus' authority over the chaos in nature and in man. To Luke, the miracles of Jesus are all miracles of the kingdom—God's sovereignty breaking in with new effectiveness upon a rebellious world. Throughout the Old Testament the sea is the symbol of those hostile forces which have not yet been brought under the rule of God. To the awed question, "Who then is this?" the answer is, it is he to whom God has entrusted the authority of his kingdom.

Luke the physician gives us all the authentic symptoms of that madman of Gerasa: morbid preoccupation with graves, abnormal strength, insensitivity to pain, refusal to wear clothes. The man considered himself inhabited by a troop of demons. In the

presence of the authority of the kingdom the poor fellow is so convulsed as the demons are exorcised that a nearby herd of pigs
stampedes off a cliff into the sea. To the onlookers it is quite evident that the unclean spirits had entered the unclean beasts and
returned to the abyss, and they are certain this has taken place
with the consent of Jesus. No wonder the natives are afraid; the
awesome presence and power of the divine are too much for
them.

8:22–39

22 One day he got into a boat with his disciples, and
he said to them, "Let us go across to the other side of
the lake." So they set out, 23 and as they sailed he fell
asleep. And a storm of wind came down on the lake,
and they were filling with water, and were in danger. 24
And they went and woke him, saying, "Master, Master,
we are perishing!" And he awoke and rebuked the wind
and the raging waves; and they ceased, and there was a
calm. 25 He said to them, "Where is your faith?" And
they were afraid, and they marveled, saying to one
another, "Who then is this, that he commands even
wind and water, and they obey him?"

26 Then they arrived at the country of the Gerasenes,
which is opposite Galilee. 27 And as he stepped out on
land, there met him a man from the city who had
demons; for a long time he had worn no clothes, and he
lived not in a house but among the tombs. 28 When he
saw Jesus, he cried out and fell down before him, and
said with a loud voice, "What have you to do with me,
Jesus, Son of the Most High God? I beseech you, do not
torment me." 29 For he had commanded the unclean
spirit to come out of the man. (For many a time it had
seized him; he was kept under guard, and bound with
chains and fetters, but he broke the bonds and was
driven by the demon into the desert.) 30 Jesus then

asked him, "What is your name?" And he said, "Legion"; for many demons had entered him. 31 And they begged him not to command them to depart into the abyss. 32 Now a large herd of swine was feeding there on the hillside; and they begged him to let them enter these. So he gave them leave. 33 Then the demons came out of the man and entered the swine, and the herd rushed down the steep bank into the lake and were drowned.

34 When the herdsmen saw what had happened, they fled, and told it in the city and in the country. 35 Then people went out to see what had happened, and they came to Jesus, and found the man from whom the demons had gone, sitting at the feet of Jesus, clothed and in his right mind; and they were afraid. 36 And those who had seen it told them how he who had been possessed with demons was healed. 37 Then all the people of the surrounding country of the Gerasenes asked him to depart from them; for they were seized with great fear; so he got into the boat and returned. 38 The man from whom the demons had gone begged that he might be with him; but he sent him away, saying, 39 "Return to your home, and declare how much God has done for you." And he went away, proclaiming throughout the whole city how much Jesus had done for him.

The good news of the kingdom of God is also demonstrated by Jesus' authority over sickness and death. The crowd which Jesus had attracted earlier has patiently awaited his return across the lake. Among them is a distraught father whose only daughter is dying. He is Jairus, president of the local synagogue, which indicates that not all religious leaders were opposed to Jesus. It must have required both courage and humility on his part to approach Jesus in view of the way most of his colleagues felt about him. Before Jesus had reached his house the child died. But in the presence of Christ death becomes "a sleeping." The good news is that if we "believe," we need not live in dread. "Do not fear," was Jesus' word to that upset father. Death must yield to the powers of the messianic kingdom present in Jesus.

En route to Jairus' house a chronically ill woman, whose embarrassing affliction made her ceremonially unclean and therefore unfit for any human contact (Lev. 15:19-30), comes behind Jesus in the crowd, touches him, and is healed. The story is saying that Jesus knows that spiritual energy has gone out of him. Every healing costs him spiritual energy which will need to be renewed in prayer. He insists on knowing her identity not in order to embarrass her, but because she needs his blessing on the cure she has gained by stealth. She needs to know that what had happened to her is not magic or mechanical, rather it is the result of her faith in the saving power of God.

8:40–56

40 Now when Jesus returned, the crowd welcomed him, for they were all waiting for him. 41 And there came a man named Jairus, who was a ruler of the synagogue; and falling at Jesus' feet he besought him to come to his house, 42 for he had an only daughter, about twelve years of age, and she was dying.

As he went, the people pressed round him. 43 And a woman who had had a flow of blood for twelve years and could not be healed by any one, 44 came up behind him, and touched the fringe of his garment; and immediately her flow of blood ceased. 45 And Jesus said, "Who was it that touched me?" When all denied it, Peter said, "Master, the multitudes surround you and press upon you!" 46 But Jesus said, "Some one touched me; for I perceive that power has gone forth from me." 47 And when the woman saw that she was not hidden, she came trembling, and falling down before him declared in the presence of all the people why she had touched him, and how she had been immediately healed. 48 And he said to her, "Daughter, your faith has made you well; go in peace."

49 While he was still speaking, a man from the ruler's house came and said, "Your daughter is dead; do not trouble the Teacher any more." 50 But Jesus on hearing this answered him, "Do not fear; only believe, and she shall be well." 51 And when he came to the house, he permitted no one to enter with him, except Peter and John and James, and the father and mother of the child. 52 And all were weeping and bewailing her; but he said, "Do not weep; for she is not dead but sleeping." 53 And they laughed at him, knowing that she was dead. 54 But taking her by the hand he called, saying, "Child, arise." 55 And her spirit returned, and she got up at once; and he directed that something should be given her to eat. 56 And her parents were amazed; but he charged them to tell no one what had happened.

In all these incidents, faith is the response through which the benefits of the kingdom are given. In each case there is some faith, if only a little, but that is mixed with a considerable amount of unfaith: the unproductive soils, the skeptical brothers of Jesus, the fearful disciples in the storm, the rejecting Gerasenes, the doubtful Peter, the jeering mourners. The note of rejection is loudly struck, but there is still the faint, clear tinkle of the chime of faith. That is the story in Galilee, and, Luke implies, such will be its destiny in the world.

A Messianic Banquet

While we are inclined to think of Jesus as a lone figure with disciples following at some distance, he thinks of himself as the head of a team. He is the agent of the kingdom and they are his associates in proclaiming it. He is inaugurating the New Israel and they are its first citizens. The demands of the crowds which he attracts plus the number of towns and villages where the good news of the kingdom has not yet been proclaimed cause a change of procedure in Jesus' Galilean ministry. He sends forth The Twelve "with power and authority . . . to preach the kingdom of God and to heal." The instructions he gives them indicate the need for haste. In spite of the large crowds which follow him as though he were a pied piper, the news of the murder of John the Baptist by Herod gives Jesus a premonition of the fate in store for him. Time is running out.

When the disciples return from their maiden missionary efforts Jesus takes them to a safe and "lonely place" near Bethsaida. It is across the border out of Galilee, Herod's jurisdiction, in the tetrarchy of Trachonitis where curious and vengeful Herod cannot reach him. No doubt this is done so that the disciples may report to Jesus and pray with him and rest. But they are interrupted. The crowds learn where they have gone and follow them around the northern end of the lake.

After Jesus had addressed them and healed many, the disciples want to send the people away, but Jesus says, "No, you give them something to eat." Then follows the most recounted incident of the four Gospels — the feeding of the five thousand. And the reason it gets so much attention is that this climax of the Galilean ministry is seen as the prototype of the messianic banquet, the coronation feast of God in his coming kingdom. The account is told in eucharistic language — "taking the five loaves and the two fish he looked up to heaven, and blessed and broke them, and gave them to the disciples to set before the crowd." The early Christians could not think of it in any other way.

9:1–17

> And he called the twelve together and gave them power and authority over all demons and to cure diseases, 2 and he sent them out to preach the kingdom of God and to heal. 3 And he said to them, "Take nothing for your journey, no staff, nor bag, nor bread, nor money; and do not have two tunics. 4 And whatever house you enter, stay there, and from there depart. 5 And wherever they do not receive you, when you leave

that city shake off the dust from your feet as a testimony against them." 6 And they departed and went through the villages, preaching the gospel and healing everywhere.

7 Now Herod the tetrarch heard of all that was done, and he was perplexed, because it was said by some that John had been raised from the dead, 8 by some that Elijah had appeared, and by others that one of the old prophets had risen. 9 Herod said, "John I beheaded; but who is this about whom I hear such things?" And he sought to see him.

10 On their return the apostles told him what they had done. And he took them and withdrew apart to a city called Bethsaida. 11 When the crowds learned it, they followed him; and he welcomed them and spoke to them of the kingdom of God, and cured those who had need of healing. 12 Now the day began to wear away; and the twelve came and said to him, "Send the crowd away, to go into the villages and country round about, to lodge and get provisions; for we are here in a lonely place." 13 But he said to them, "You give them something to eat." They said, "We have no more than five loaves and two fish—unless we are to go and buy food for all these people." 14 For there were about five thousand men. And he said to his diciples, "Make them sit down in companies, about fifty each." 15 And they did so, and made them all sit down. 16 And taking the five loaves and the two fish he looked up to heaven, and blessed and broke them, and gave them to the disciples to set before the crowd. 17 And all ate and were satisfied. And they took up what was left over, twelve baskets of broken pieces.

None of the accounts of this incident in the four Gospels *say* that Jesus multiplied the loaves. The miracle only enters at cleanup time. The point is that the remembered importance of the occasion lies in the impressive act of prophetic symbolism, not in analyzing, rationalizing, or questioning a miracle of multiplication.

"This is My Son; Listen to Him"

Luke dramatically builds up the reader's quest for the true identity of Jesus. The amazed disciples in the storm-tossed boat asked themselves, "Who is this?" Herod reiterates the same question and guesses the wrong answer—resurrected John the Baptist. Now Jesus asks the disciples for their answer. People were guessing: John the Baptist returned? Elijah? Some other ancient prophet? Peter shows how much the insight of the disciples has deepened: "You are God's Messiah." The purpose of the Galilean ministry has been accomplished. Jesus immediately begins to add new content to that ancient title.

Through his meditations on the Scriptures, Jesus had come to the conclusion that his role was that of a fusion of three Old Testament figures—the Messiah, the Son of man, and the Servant of the Lord. The Messiah was the Davidic king in whose reign God's justice and peace would be restored. The Son of man was the symbolic heavenly figure of Daniel's vision (Dan. 7:13), identified with the rewarding of the persecuted saints of the Most High. The Servant of the Lord was Israel or a faithful remnant which through vicarious suffering and death would bring the nations to the knowledge of God (Isa. 52:13–53:12). In Jesus' blending of these roles, primary importance is given to the establishment of God's kingdom and the realization of Israel's destiny as the holy People of God. He, the Messiah, and ultimately his faithful followers, must suffer. This is the way in which they will bring God's redemption to the world. "The Son of man *must* suffer . . . ." "If any man would come after me, let him deny himself and take up his cross daily and follow me." These were hard insights to come by, hard lessons to learn.

The disciples are still struggling with them a week later when Jesus takes his three most intimate disciples with him up on a mountain to pray. Jesus is wrestling with the triple insight he seeks to convey to them: the Messiah must suffer, his disciples must be prepared to share his suffering, and his suffering and theirs must be seen in the context of ultimate glory. It is an occasion of creative inspiration. In their sleepy half-wakefulness on that misty, mountain-top morning, the disciples are caught up in their Lord's vision. Moses and Elijah, venerable representatives of Israel's past, talk with Jesus about his death at Jerusalem which every day is becoming a more imminent prospect. Peter wants to freeze that moment of spiritual summitry — build three booths — without realizing that Moses and Elijah, along with John the Baptist, are part of the old passing age and are now succeeded by Jesus. The voice from heaven — God's voice — sets him straight: "This is my Son, my Chosen; *listen to him!*" The heavenly voice at the time of Jesus' baptism had confirmed his messiahship for him. Now the same voice confirms that truth for the disciples. They are profoundly moved as their reaction of silence attests.

The main interest in what takes place when Jesus and the disciples come down from the mountain lies in Jesus' impatient boiling over at the ineptness of his followers, "How long am I to be with you?" We sence a new urgency here. The showdown in Jerusalem moves closer by the day and he is irritated with the slowness of his disciples. They are no more prepared for his second announcement of his coming passion than they were for the first. "They did not understand . . . and they were afraid to ask him."

Two little incidents become the occasion for Jesus to teach more of the meaning of the cross and the nature of true greatness. The disciples are squabbling among themselves about who is greatest. Jesus sets humble service above preeminence and makes it clear that every loyal follower is welcome.

With these stories the Galilean mission comes to a close on a negative note: even those who recognize him as the Messiah find the nature of his mission and of his kingdom beyond their comprehension.

18 Now it happened that as he was praying alone the disciples were with him; and he asked them, "Who do the people say that I am?" 19 And they answered, "John the Baptist; but others say, Elijah; and others, that one of the old prophets has risen." 20 And he said to them, "But who do you say that I am?" And Peter answered, "The Christ of God." 21 But he charged and commanded them to tell this to no one, 22 saying, "The Son of man must suffer many things, and be rejected by the elders and chief priests and scribes, and be killed, and on the third day be raised."

23 And he said to all, "If any man would come after me, let him deny himself and take up his cross daily and follow me. 24 For whoever would save his life will lose it; and whoever loses his life for my sake, he will save it. 25 For what does it profit a man if he gains the whole world and loses or forfeits himself? 26 For whoever is ashamed of me and of my words, of him will the Son of man be ashamed when he comes in his glory and the glory of the Father and of the holy angels. 27 But I tell you truly, there are some standing here who will not taste death before they see the kingdom of God."

28 Now about eight days after these sayings he took with him Peter and John and James, and went up on the mountain to pray. 29 And as he was praying, the appearance of his countenance was altered, and his raiment became dazzling white. 30 And behold, two men talked with him, Moses and Elijah, 31 who appeared in glory and spoke of his departure, which he was to accomplish at Jerusalem. 32 Now Peter and those who were with him were very heavy with sleep, and when they wakened they saw his glory and the two men who stood with him. 33 And as the men were parting from

him, Peter said to Jesus, "Master, it is well that we are here; let us make three booths, one for you and one for Moses and one for Elijah" — not knowing what he said. 34 As he said this, a cloud came and overshadowed them; and they were afraid as they entered the cloud. 35 And a voice came out of the cloud, saying, "This is my Son, my Chosen; listen to him!" 36 And when the voice had spoken, Jesus was found alone. And they kept silence and told no one in those days anything of what they had seen.

37 On the next day, when they had come down from the mountain, a great crowd met him. 38 And behold, a man from the crowd cried, Teacher, I beg you to look upon my son, for he is my only child; 39 and behold, a spirit seizes him, and he suddenly cries out; it convulses him till he foams, and shatters him, and will hardly leave him. And I begged your disciples to cast it out, but they could not. 41 Jesus answered, "O faithless and perverse generation, how long am I to be with you and bear with you? Bring your son here." 42 While he was coming, the demon tore him and convulsed him. But Jesus rebuked the unclean spirit, and healed the boy, and gave him back to his father. 43 And all were astonished at the majesty of God.

But while they were all marveling at everything he did, he said to his diciples, 44 "Let these words sink into your ears; for the Son of man is to be delivered into the hands of men." 45 But they did not understand this saying, and it was concealed from them, that they should not perceive it; and they were afraid to ask him about this saying.

46 And an argument arose among them as to which of them was the greatest. 47 But when Jesus perceived the thought of their hearts, he took a child and put him by his side, 48 and said to them, "Whoever receives this child in my name receives me, and whoever receives me

receives him who sent me; for he who is least among you all is the one who is great."

49 John answered, "Master, we saw a man casting out demons in your name, and we forbade him, because he does not follow with us." 50 But Jesus said to him, "Do not forbid him; for he that is not against you is for you."

The Transfiguration account is filled with symbolism. As we have seen earlier, a mountain, to Luke, is always the place of revelation and of communion with God. The "glory" associated with the appearance of Moses and Elijah is the New Testament way to describe the reality of the presence of the new age. Those two Old Testament personages speak with Jesus about "his departure" (literally, his "exodus"). Probably the whole of his redemptive work is implied — death, resurrection, and ascension. Jesus, the new Moses, will establish the New Israel, give a new covenant, and through his death and resurrection deliver God's people from their "Egyptian" slavery to sin and death. This is the symbolism Luke's readers are intended to grasp.

It is characteristic of Luke to provide a transition piece from one part of his Gospel to the next. The Transfiguration is both a highlight at the close of the Galilean ministry and the occasion which turns our attention toward Jerusalem and the approaching time of the Lord's suffering, death, and resurrection. The freer days of large, friendly crowds and great popularity are over. There are dark, menacing clouds on the southern horizon. That is the direction of Jerusalem. That is the road Jesus and the disciples are now about to travel.

CHAPTER 5

JOURNEY TO JERUSALEM

"When the days drew near for Jesus to be received up, he set his face to go to Jerusalem." So begins the "journey" section, 9:51-19:28, of Luke's Gospel. In the words "to be received up," Luke is saying that everything now points toward the Lord's victorious climax — death, resurrection, and ascension. (In John's Gospel "glorified" carries this same three-fold meaning, John 12:16, 23.)

The "journey" starts as Jesus and The Twelve enter a Samaritan village. There was a long-standing feud between the Jews and the Samaritans. It was racial, political, and religious, and was symbolized by their rival temples of Jerusalem and Mount Gerizim. Samaritan antipathy came out most strongly against Jews who were on pilgrimage to Jerusalem. Rather than cursing and destroying those who were his enemies, as Elijah had done (2 Kings 1:9-16), Jesus' behavior was something new. As the Transfiguration made clear, Jesus had superseded Elijah and his new way was that of loving his enemies and dying for them.

The sending out of the "seventy others" was, like the sending out of The Twelve earlier, in order to heal in the Lord's Name and to preach the kingdom. The instructions were similar to those The Twelve had received, but in more detail. They are probably the kind of instructions the post-resurrection Church gave the early Christian missionaries as they were sent out in twos. The sending out of seventy is also part of Luke's symbolism. Moses shared his burden in ministering to the children of Israel with seventy assistants (Num. 11:16-17). Now Jesus, the new Moses, has a similar number ministering to the New Israel.

Their success, like that of Jesus, is mixed, as his condemnation of Chorazin and Bethsaida makes clear. But even so, the earthly victories of those faithful to the kingdom reflect the heavenly victory of the King of kings over Satan, and the ultimate triumph of good over evil. The Lord's exultant messianic thanksgiving is both because of this foretaste of God's ultimate victory, and of the inclusion of his faithful ones in that glorious insight.

9:51–56

> 51 When the days drew near for him to be received up, he set his face to go to Jerusalem. And he sent messengers ahead of him, 52 who went and entered a village of the Samaritans, to make ready for him; 53 but the people would not receive him, because his face was set toward Jerusalem. 54 And when his disciples James and John saw it, they said, "Lord, do you want us to bid fire come down from heaven and consume them?" 55 But he turned and rebuked them. 56 And they went on to another village . . . .

10:1–6

> After this the Lord appointed seventy others, and sent them on ahead of him, two by two, into every town and place where he himself was about to come. 2 And he said to them, "The harvest is plentiful, but the laborers are few; pray therefore the Lord of the harvest to send out laborers into his harvest. 3 Go your way; behold, I send you out as lambs in the midst of wolves. 4 Carry no purse, no bag, no sandals; and salute no one on the road. 5 Whatever house you enter, first say, 'Peace be to this house!' 6 And if a son of peace is there, your peace shall rest upon him; but if not, it shall return to you . . . .

13"Woe to you, Chorazin! woe to you, Bethsaida! For if the mighty works done in you had been done in Tyre and Sidon, they would have repented long ago, sitting in sackcloth and ashes. 14 But it shall be more tolerable in the judgment for Tyre and Sidon than for you. 15 And you, Capernaum, will you be exalted to heaven? You shall be brought down to Hades.

16 "He who hears you hears me, and he who rejects you rejects me, and he who rejects me rejects him who sent me."

17 The seventy returned with joy, saying, "Lord, even the demons are subject to us in your name!" 18 And he said to them, "I saw Satan fall like lightning from heaven. 19 Behold, I have given you authority to tread upon serpents and scorpions, and over all the power of the enemy; and nothing shall hurt you. 20 Nevertheless do not rejoice in this, that the spirits are subject to you; but rejoice that your names are written in heaven."

21 In that same hour he rejoiced in the Holy Spirit and said, "I thank thee, Father, Lord of heaven and earth, that thou hast hidden these things from the wise and understanding and revealed them to babes; yea, Father, for such was thy gracious will. 22 All things have been delivered to me by my Father; and no one knows who the Son is except the Father, or who the Father is except the Son and any one to whom the Son chooses to reveal him."

23 Then turning to the disciples he said privately, "Blessed are the eyes which see what you see! 24 For I tell you that many prophets and kings desired to see what you see, and did not see it, and to hear what you hear, and did not hear it."

The "journey" to Jerusalem is a Lucan contrivance. It is a section that contains a great deal of teaching, but do not attempt to follow it on the map. Luke was an outsider and did not know the territory. The opening paragraph of the section is very definitely about a journey, but subsequent geographic references are bafflingly misleading and the time sequence is equally confusing. It is best to think of the section as part of the pattern of this Gospel in which everything said and done is under the shadow of Jesus' coming confrontation with the religious authorities in Jerusalem, and moves in that direction. The author preserves the dramatic tension of his story by constant reminders of the crisis that lies ahead.

The Good Samaritan

The incidents during the beginning of the "journey" all put meaning into the word discipleship. We saw it in Jesus' dealing with the vengeful disciples in the Samaritan village, and saw it in his instructions to the seventy. Now a lawyer provides a new occasion for further teaching on the subject. The encounter contains legalistic sparring. It begins with the lawyer's sneaky question which is intended to put Jesus on the spot regarding his knowledge of Scripture. Jesus cleverly puts the lawyer on the defensive. But the lawyer then seeks to involve Jesus in an age-old debate. He wants Jesus to set limits on one's moral duty; like all of the Pharisees he wants proper behavior carefully, legally defined. Jesus declines to set any limits on love. The lawyer wants a precise answer to the question, "Who is my neighbor?" Jesus' parable of the Good Samaritan rephrases the question: "To whom can I be a neighbor?" And, of course, the answer one draws from the parable is, "To anyone whose need constitutes a claim on my love." The point of view which determines how one behaves is that of the man in the ditch: "As you wish that men would do to you, do so to them" (6:31). So the Golden Rule is graphically explained.

The Martha-Mary incident is included here as a gentle warning to disciples against self-pity and self-concern.

25 And behold, a lawyer stood up to put him to the test, saying, "Teacher, what shall I do to inherit eternal life?" 26 He said to him, "What is written in the law? How do you read?" 27 And he answered, "You shall love the Lord your God with all your heart, and with all your soul, and with all your strength, and with all your mind; and your neighbor as yourself." 28 And he said to him, "You have answered right; do this, and you will live."

29 But he, desiring to justify himself, said to Jesus, "And who is my neighbor?" 30 Jesus replied, "A man was going down from Jerusalem to Jericho, and he fell among robbers, who stripped him and beat him, and departed, leaving him half-dead. 31 Now by chance a priest was going down that road; and when he saw him he passed by on the other side. 32 So likewise a Levite, when he came to the place and saw him, passed by on the other side. 33 But a Samaritan, as he journeyed, came to where he was; and when he saw him, he had compassion, 34 and went to him and bound up his wounds, pouring on oil and wine; then he set him on his own beast and brought him to an inn, and took care of him. 35 And the next day he took out two denarii and gave them to the innkeeper, saying, 'Take care of him; and whatever more you spend, I will repay you when I come back.' 36 Which of these three, do you think, proved neighbor to the man who fell among robbers?" 37 He said, "The one who showed mercy on him." And Jesus said to him, "Go and do likewise."

38 Now as they went on their way, he entered a village; and a woman named Martha received him into her house. 39 And she had a sister called Mary, who sat at the Lord's feet and listened to his teaching. 40 But Martha was distracted with much serving; and she went

to him and said, "Lord, do you not care that my sister has left me to serve alone? Tell her then to help me." 41 But the Lord answsered her, "Martha, Martha, you are anxious and troubled about many things; 42 one thing is needful. Mary has chosen the good portion, which shall not be taken away from her."

In Mark, Jesus puts Deuteronomy 6:5 and Leviticus 19:18 side by side to produce the Summary of the Law (Mk. 12:28-32). Luke is probably correct that the rabbis had long since coupled those two verses into that classic formula for behavior.

The Martha-Mary story gets overplayed in Mary's favor. Martha is the central figure. Because Luke places the story right after the Good Samaritan, Martha, the hostess, is seen as demonstrating unselfish service, rather than as seeking her own pleasure. The Lord's reproof, however, is a gentle warning that good works need to be tempered with self-forgetfulness, otherwise the doer is likely to pour bile instead of balm on the moment.

The Lord's Prayer and the Lord's Opponents

Building substance into the meaning of discipleship continues with the Lord's teaching on prayer. In response to the disciples' request Jesus teaches them what has become the most universally used Christian prayer. The Lord's Prayer, whether Luke's version or Matthew's, covers all that a child needs to say to the Heavenly Father. God is honored, his will and goals are prayed for, then come petitions for one's individual needs: bread for the day, forgiveness to the extent to which we are able to receive it, and protection from any trial which would be too much for our strength of character. The parable and accompanying comments which enlarge our understanding of prayer make it clear that God's children must persist in the confidence that God knows what is best; he knows what he is about.

The emphasis now shifts from discipleship to kinds of opposition which are roadblocks to the work of the kingdom. As Jesus is freeing a person from demon possession he is accused of being in league with the devil. No, says Jesus, Satan would not cooperate in his own downfall. Another fatal attitude is the desire for a "sign from heaven" — exorcism of evil spirits is not spectacular enough. Again Jesus rejects shallow curiosity as he had rejected a similar temptation in the wilderness before his ministry began. Then comes a considerable denunciation of the hypocrisy of the Pharisees. Luke has this take place on one of the occasions when Jesus is dining in a Pharisee's home. This is an unlikely setting and the series of "woes" probably was not all spoken on any one occasion regardless of Luke's arrangement.

11:1–20

He was praying in a certain place, and when he ceased, one of his disciples said to him, "Lord, teach us to pray, as John taught his disciples." 2 And he said to them, "When you pray, say:

"Father, hallowed be thy name. Thy kingdom come. 3 Give us each day our daily bread; 4 and forgive us our sins, for we ourselves forgive every one who is indebted to us; and lead us not into temptation."

5 And he said to them, "Which of you who has a friend will go to him at midnight and say to him, 'Friend, lend me three loaves; 6 for a friend of mine has arrived on a journey, and I have nothing to set before him'; 7 and he will answer from within, 'Do not bother me; the door is now shut, and my children are with me in bed; I cannot get up and give you anything'? 8 I tell you, though he will not get up and give him anything because he is his friend, yet because of his importunity he will rise and give him whatever he needs. 9 And I tell you, Ask, and it will be given you; seek, and you will find; knock, and it will be opened to you. 10 For every one who asks receives, and he who seeks finds, and to him who knocks it will be opened. 11 What Father among you, if his son asks for a fish, will instead of a fish give him a serpent; 12 or if he asks for an egg, will give

him a scorpion? 13 If you then, who are evil, know how to give good gifts to your children, how much more will the heavenly Father give the Holy Spirit to those who ask him?"

14 Now he was casting out a demon that was dumb; when the demon had gone out, the dumb man spoke, and the people marveled. 15 But some of them said, "He casts out demons by Beelzebul, the prince of demons"; 16 while others, to test him, sought from him a sign from heaven. 17 But he, knowing their thoughts, said to them, "Every kingdom divided against itself is laid waste, and a divided household falls. 18 And if Satan also is divided against himself, how will his kingdom stand? For you say that I cast out demons by Beelzebul. 19 And if I cast out demons by Beelzebul, by whom do your sons cast them out? Therefore they shall be your judges. 20 But if it is by the finger of God that I cast out demons, then the kingdom of God has come upon you . . . . "

11:29–30

29 When the crowds were increasing, he began to say, "This generation is an evil generation; it seeks a sign, but no sign shall be given to it except the sign of Jonah. 30 For as Jonah became a sign to the men of Nineveh, so will the Son of man be to this generation . . . . "

11:37–54

37 While he was speaking, a Pharisee asked him to dine with him; so he went in and sat at table. 38 The Pharisee was astonished to see that he did not first wash before dinner. 39 And the Lord said to him, "Now you Pharisees cleanse the outside of the cup and

of the dish, but inside you are full of extortion and wickedness. 40 You fools! Did not he who made the outside make the inside also? 41 But give for alms those things which are within; and behold, everything is clean for you.

42 But woe to you Pharisees! For you tithe mint and rue and every herb, and neglect justice and the love of God; these you ought to have done without neglecting the others. 43 Woe to you Pharisees! For you love the best seats in synagogues and salutations in the market places. 44 Woe to you! For you are like graves which are not seen, and men walk over them without knowing it."

45 One of the lawyers answered him, "Teacher, in saying this you reproach us also." 46 And he said, "Woe to you lawyers also! For you load men with burdens hard to bear, and you yourselves do not touch the burdens with one of your fingers. 47 Woe to you! For you build the tombs of the prophets whom your fathers killed. 48 So you are witnesses and consent to the deeds of your fathers; for they killed them, and you build their tombs. 49 Therefore also the Wisdom of God said, 'I will send them prophets and apostles, some of whom they will kill and persecute,' 50 that the blood of all the prophets, shed from the foundation of the world, may be required of this generation, 51 from the blood of Abel to the blood of Zechariah, who perished between the altar and the sanctuary. Yes, I tell you, it shall be required of this generation. 52 Woe to you lawyers! For you have taken away the key of knowledge; you did not enter yourselves, and you hindered those who were entering."

53 As he went away from there, the scribes and the Pharisees began to press him hard, and to provoke him to speak of many things, 54 lying in wait for him, to catch at something he might say.

12:1

> In the meantime, when so many thousands of the multitude had gathered together that they trod upon one another, he began to say to his disciples first, "Beware of the leaven of the Pharisees, which is hypocrisy . . . . "

This version of the Lord's Prayer is probably nearer the original than Matthew's more elaborate one (Mt. 6:9–13). The Lucan setting — in response to the disciples' request — is also more likely than as part of a great sermon as in Matthew.

The Pharisees were an influential politico-religious party that advocated a segregated Jewish culture, looked for a political Messiah, and stressed strict adherence to a rabbinical interpretation of the Law as set forth in the Old Testament. The scribes made the copies of the manuscripts containing the Law. They therefore knew the Law; hence, they were the lawyers. Most of them were members of the Pharisaic party.

Notice that Jesus' popularity continues to grow, but the opposition to him does also. The Pharisees and their colleagues do not approve of Jesus' "loose" interpretation of the Law. They hate the obvious authority with which he speaks and the way he openly criticizes the gulf between their public pronouncements and their personal practice. He is a threat. He is an embarrassment. He must be gotten rid of as soon as possible. So they are "lying in wait for him, to catch at something he might say" for which he can be arrested.

In Jesus' diatribe against the Pharisees notice that he never condemns all Pharisees. Rather he sees that as a group they were more prone to hypocrisy than others because of the nature of their teaching. Hypocrisy is masquerade. The person one sees is not the real self. He is fooling, and he may not even realize it. Appearance has displaced the truth. However, while he and others may be taken in by his charade, God is not fooled. The hypocrite is not as good or as noble or as kind as he pretends and the day will come when all his pretense will be exposed. The opposite of hypocrisy is repentance, which means accepting the truth about one's self, admitting what one is really like.

About Security

The next teaching deals with the matter of true and false security. The Parable of the Rich Fool is played to the drum beat of "my . . . my . . . my . . . my . . . my . . ." and the man finds out too late that the real owner is not "me" but God, and the only possession worth striving for is that which death cannot take from him.

The Lord's succeeding comments make it clear that nothing so distracts one from whole-hearted devotion to the kingdom as worry. Pagans fail to realize that the Heavenly Father cares about and provides for his children. Look, says Jesus, at the evidences of God's fatherly love in the world of nature.

12:13–31

13 One of the multitude said to him, "Teacher, bid my brother divide the inheritance with me." 14 But he said to him, "Man, who made me a judge or divider over you?" 15 And he said to them, "Take heed, and beware of all covetousness; for a man's life does not consist in the abundance of his possessions." 16 And he told them a parable, saying, "The land of a rich man brought forth plentifully; 17 and he thought to himself, 'What shall I do, for I have nowhere to store my crops?' 18 And he said, 'I will do this: I will pull down my barns, and build larger ones; and there I will store all my grain and my goods. 19 And I will say to my soul, Soul, you have ample goods laid up for many years; take your ease, eat, drink, be merry.' 20 But God said to him, 'Fool! This night your soul is required of you; and the things you have prepared, whose will they be?' 21 So is he who lays up treasure for himself, and is not rich toward God."

22 And he said to his disciples, "Therefore I tell you, do not be anxious about your life, what you shall eat, nor about your body, what you shall put on. 23 For life is more than food, and the body more than clothing. 24 Consider the ravens: they neither sow nor reap, they have neither storehouse nor barn, and yet God feeds them. Of how much more value are you than the birds! 25 And which of you by being anxious can add a cubit to his span of life? 26 If then you are not able to do as small a thing as that, why are you anxious about the rest? 27 Consider the lilies, how they grow; they neither toil nor spin; yet I tell you, even Solomon in all his glory was not arrayed like one of these. 28 But if God so clothes the grass which is alive in the field today and tomorrow is thrown into the oven, how much more will he clothe you, O men of little faith? 29 And do not seek what you are to eat and what you are to drink, nor be of anxious mind. 30 For all the nations of the world seek these things; and your Father knows that you need them. 31 Instead seek his kingdom, and these things shall be yours as well . . . . "

The Parable of the Rich Fool, like so many of the parables in the "journey" section, probably comes from Luke's special source "L." The admonition against anxiety with its illustrations from nature comes from the "Q" source which Matthew and Luke both use. Matthew incorporates it in the Sermon on the Mount (Mt. 6:25ff).

Evidence of the Coming Crisis

Jesus thinks of the coming crisis at Jerusalem as in a sense three-fold. It will, of course, mean his death, but it will also involve a searching test of his disciples, and judgment for Israel. So we have a series of warnings about the impending emergency. First to the disciples:

12:35-40

> "35 Let your loins be girded and your lamps burning,
> 36 and be like men who are waiting for their master to
> come home from the marriage feast, so that they may
> open to him at once when he comes and knocks. 37
> Blessed are those servants whom the master finds awake
> when he comes; truly, I say to you, he will gird himself
> and have them sit at table and come and serve them. 38
> If he comes in the second watch, or in the third, and
> find them so, blessed are those servants! 39But know
> this, that if the householder had known at what hour
> the thief was coming, he would not have left his house
> to be broken into. 40 You also must be ready; for the
> son of man is coming at an unexpected hour . . . . "

In speaking of that crisis as applied to himself Jesus gives us a
glimpse of his inmost thoughts and we see a mixture of impa-
tience and reluctance.

12:49-53

> 49 "I came to cast fire upon the earth; and would
> that it were already kindled! 50 I have a baptism to be
> baptized with; and how I am constrained until it is ac-
> complished! 51 Do you think that I have come to give
> peace on earth? No, I tell you, but rather division; 52
> for henceforth in one house there will be five divided,
> three against two and two against three; 53 they will be
> divided, father against son and son against father,
> mother against daughter and daughter against her
> mother, mother-in-law against her daughter-in-law
> and daughter-in-law against her mother-in-law."

The people of Israel were blind to the coming crisis and un-
aware of the judgment which it would entail. Jesus attempts to
jolt them into alert concern.

12:54-56

> 54 He also said to the multitudes, "When you see a
> cloud rising in the west, you say at once, 'A shower is

coming'; and so it happens. 55 And when you see the south wind blowing, you say, 'There will be scorching heat'; and it happens. 56 You hypocrites! You know how to interpret the appearance of earth and sky; but why do you not know how to interpret the present time? . . . "

13:1–5

There were some present at that very time who told him of the Galileans whose blood Pilate had mingled with their sacrifices. 2 And he answered them, "Do you think that these Galileans were worse sinners than all the other Galileans, because they suffered thus? 3 I tell you, No; but unless you repent you will all likewise perish. 4 Or those eighteen upon whom the tower in Siloam fell and killed them, do you think that they were worse offenders than all the others who dwelt in Jerusalem? 5 I tell you, No; but unless you repent you will all likewise perish." . . .

Now follow two brushes with unfriendly Pharisees. The first sounds like similar experiences during Jesus' ministry in Galilee. He is teaching in a synagogue on the Sabbath. There is an afflicted woman present; in his instinctive compassion he heals her. The ruler of the synagogue is "indignant because Jesus had healed on the Sabbath." (Only if a person's life is in danger is this permissible.) Jesus acts in response to a necessity which takes precedence over all other obligations, including the Sabbath Law — the necessity of pity, caring, love. His similar encounters at an earlier date had to do with the Messiah's authority over the Sabbath (6:1–10). On this occasion it is the Messiah's teaching about the meaning of the Sabbath.

The second encounter is with Pharisees who pose as friends warning Jesus to leave Herod's jurisdiction. Herod had rightly gained the nickname "The Fox." Jesus was a problem to him because of his effect on the people. He dared not arrest so popular a person so he sought to drive him from his tetrarchy in this devious way — supposed friends warning him of danger. Jesus sees through the ruse and his reaction is filled with contempt. A smalltime politician will never usurp the tragic historic role of Jerusalem as killer of the prophets. Then in a swift change of mood comes his poignant lament over the Godforsaken city.

13:10-19

10 Now he was teaching in one of the synagogues on the sabbath. 11 And there was a woman who had had a spirit of infirmity for eighteen years; she was bent over and could not fully straighten herself. 12 And when Jesus saw her, he called her and said to her, "Woman, you are freed from your infirmity." 13 And he laid his hands upon her, and immediately she was made straight, and she praised God. 14 But the ruler of the synagogue, indignant because Jesus had healed on the sabbath, said to the people, "There are six days on which work ought to be done; come on those days and be healed, and not on the sabbath day." 15 Then the Lord answered him, "You hypocrites! Does not each of you on the sabbath untie his ox or his ass from the manager, and lead it away to water it? 16 And ought not this woman, a daughter of Abraham whom Satan bound for eighteen years, be loosed from this bond on the sabbath day?" 17 As he said this, all his adversaries were put to shame; and all the people rejoiced at all the glorious things that were done by him.

18 He said therefore, "What is the kingdom of God like? And to what shall I compare it? 19 It is like a grain of mustard seed which a man took and sowed in his garden; and it grew and became a tree, and the birds of the air made nests in its branches." ...

13:31-35

31 At that very hour some Pharisees came, and said to him, "Get away from here, for Herod wants to kill you." 32 And he said to them, "Go and tell that fox, 'Behold, I cast out demons and perform cures today and tomorrow, and the third day I finish my course.

33 Nevertheless I must go on my way today and tomorrow and the day following; for it cannot be that a prophet should perish away from Jerusalem.' 34 O Jerusalem, Jerusalem, killing the prophets and stoning those who are sent to you! How often would I have gathered your children together as a hen gathers her brood under her wings, and you would not! 35 Behold, your house is forsaken! And I tell you, you will not see me until you say, 'Blessed is he who comes in the name of the Lord!'"

Jesus' little parable of the mustard seed is saying that he considered the kingdom of God a present reality evident in small triumphs over the victims of Satan's tyranny. The healing of the afflicted woman is an example. While such a victory seems insignificant compared to the immense power of evil, yet it is a foretaste of the kingdom's ultimate coming.

Again we see the contrast between Jesus' popularity with unimportant, rank-and-file people and the gathering cloud of opposition from people in authority like the ruler of the synagogue.

At a Pharisee's Dinner

Many of Jesus' sayings, teachings, parables came into Luke's hands with no context to indicate the occasion on which they were first said. That is true of much of the material which Luke puts in his "journey" section. In Chapter 14 a Sabbath-day dinner at the home of 'a ruler who belonged to the Pharisees" (probably a member of the Sanhedrin) becomes for Luke the occasion of a healing, of teachings on status-seeking and social climbing, and of a parable on those accepted at the banquet of God.

Jesus is saying that the law of mercy takes precedence over the law of the Sabbath. In his teaching he makes clear that heavenly blessedness comes to those who show kindness and hospitality where there is no possibility of recompense, and that none are barred from the heavenly banquet except those who disqualify themselves through finding preoccupations more attractive.

One sabbath when he went to dine at the house of a ruler who belonged to the Pharisees, they were watching him. 2 And behold, there was a man before him who had dropsy. 3 And Jesus spoke to the lawyers and Pharisees, saying, "Is it lawful to heal on the sabbath, or not?" 4 But they were silent. Then he took him and healed him, and let him go. 5 And he said to them, "Which of you, having a son or an ox that has fallen into a well, will not immediately pull him out on a sabbath day?" 6 And they could not reply to this.

7 Now he told a parable to those who were invited, when he marked how they chose the places of honor, saying to them, 8 "When you are invited by any one to a marriage feast, do not sit down in a place of honor, lest a more eminent man than you be invited by him; 9 and he who invited you both will come and say to you, 'Give place to this man,' and then you will begin with shame to take the lowest place. 10 But when you are invited, go and sit in the lowest place, so that when your host comes he may say to you, 'Friend, go up higher'; then you will be honored in the presence of all who sit at table with you. 11 For every one who exalts himself will be humbled, and he who humbles himself will be exalted."

12 He said also to the man who had invited him, "When you give a dinner or a banquet, do not invite your friends or your brothers or your kinsmen or rich neighbors, lest they also invite you in return, and you be repaid. 13 But when you give a feast, invite the poor, the maimed, the lame, the blind, 14 and you will be blessed, because they cannot repay you. You will be repaid at the resurrection of the just."

15 When one of those who sat at table with him heard this, he said to him, " Blessed is he who shall eat

bread in the kingdom of God!" 16 But he said to him, "A man once gave a great banquet, and invited many; 17 and at the time for the banquet he sent his servant to say to those who had been invited, 'Come; for all is now ready.' 18 But they all alike began to make excuses. The first said to him, 'I have bought a field, and I must go out and see it; I pray you, have me excused.' 19 And another said, 'I have bought five yoke of oxen, and I go to examine them; I pray you, have me excused.' 20 And another said, 'I have married a wife, and therefore I cannot come.' 21 So the servant came and reported this to his master. Then the householder in anger said to his servant, 'Go out quickly to the streets and lanes of the city, and bring in the poor and maimed and blind and lame.' 22 And the servant said, 'Sir, what you commanded has been done, and still there is room.' 23 And the master said to the servant, 'Go out to the highways and hedges, and compel people to come in, that my house may be filled. 24 For I tell you, none of those men who were invited shall taste my banquet.' "

What Jesus says is part of his continuing argument with the Pharisees. The Sabbath-day dinner in the Pharisee's home appears to be such an occasion — probably a staged situation. His host was a prominent defender of the Law. His other guests included "lawyers" — theologians, authorities on the Law, influential people. The man with the dropsy, a disease considered to be the result of one's immorality, just "happened" to be present? Perhaps. But in any case "they watched Jesus." He, as always, was on the side of the poor, the needy, the suffering, the helpless; they could not conceive of a loving concern for one's fellows taking precedence over the law of God as they understood it. Even though Jesus had forestalled any verbal criticism of his action on this occasion with questions which put the Pharisees on the defensive, they no doubt (as previously on a similar occasion) "were filled with fury and discussed with one another what they might do to Jesus" (6:11).

Qualifications of Discipleship

Jesus continued to have a large following of enthusiastic but uncomprehending folk. They were fascinated by what he said and did, but they did not perceive that everything he said and did was about the kingdom of God. Jesus continued to try to penetrate beyond their emotional enthusiasm to a more profound understanding of discipleship. His words here were spoken at a time when the shadow of the cross was beginning to loom very large, and the hostility of the religious authorities was becoming more and more ominous.

The Semitic way of saying "I prefer this to that" is "I like this and hate that," so Jesus is saying that ties of kinship must not be allowed to interfere with absolute commitment to the kingdom. Half-hearted commitment will not suffice; like salt, it is either good or it is no good. There is no in-between.

14:25–35

25 Now great multitudes accompanied him; and he turned and said to them, 26 "If any one comes to me and does not hate his own father and mother and wife and children and brothers and sisters, yes, and even his own life, he cannot be my disciple. 27 Whoever does not bear his own cross and come after me, cannot be my disciple. 28 For which of you, desiring to build a tower, does not first sit down and count the cost, whether he has enough to complete it? 29 Otherwise, when he has laid a foundation, and is not able to finish, all who see it begin to mock him, 30 saying, 'This man began to build, and was not able to finish.' 31 Or what king, going to encounter another king in war, will not sit down first and take counsel whether he is able with ten thousand to meet him who comes against him with twenty thousand? 32 And if not, while the other is yet a great way off, he sends an embassy and asks terms of peace. 33 So therefore, whoever of you does not renounce all that he has cannot be my disciple.

34 "Salt is good; but if salt has lost its taste, how shall its saltness be restored? 35 It is fit neither for the land nor for the dunghill; men throw it away. He who has ears to hear, let him hear."

Seeking the Lost

The Pharisees made a business of serving God correctly. Obviously, to do this they had to avoid any contact with evil; indeed, they even had to avoid the possibility of contamination through association with persons who were not as strict as they were about keeping the Law. It is like catching a cold: you can get it by permitting yourself to become run down. You may also get it by associating with a person who has it.

Jesus associated freely with outcasts who were ceremonially unclean. The Pharisees could not understand such behavior. Jesus made it clear that God does not wait for sinners to repent; rather, he takes the initiative in bringing about their restoration. Some sinners have thoughtlessly strayed like lost sheep. Some are lost like coins because of another's carelessness. Some like the prodigal son have willfully left the circle of the Father's love, and some like the elder brother are through self-conscious righteousness equally far from being true members of the Family of God.

In Jesus' three parables about the lost, that of the Lost Sheep and Lost Coin are about the poor, the afflicted, the outcast of society, and there is great joy in heaven when they are found. The two sons who took the initiative for what they did are lost in a different way. Both are willful, both are selfish, both need to realize their alienation and repent in order to enjoy being with the Father in the Father's house. Perhaps the tax-collectors are like the prodigal son, although the parable was not told to offer generous pardon to the nation's prodigals, but rather to entreat the respectable Jews to rejoice with God over the restoration of sinners.

15:1–32

Now the tax collectors and sinners were all drawing near to hear him. 2 And the Pharisees and the scribes murmured, saying, "This man receives sinners and eats with them."

3 So he told them this parable: 4 "What man of you, having a hundred sheep, if he has lost one of them, does not leave the ninety-nine in the wilderness, and go after the one which is lost, until he finds it? 5 And when he has found it, he lays it on his shoulders, rejoicing. 6 And when he comes home, he calls together his friends and his neighbors, saying to them, 'Rejoice with me, for I have found my sheep which was lost.' 7 Just so, I tell you, there will be more joy in heaven over one sinner who repents than over ninety-nine righteous persons who need not repentance.

8 "Or what woman, having ten silver coins, if she loses one coin, does not light a lamp and sweep the house and seek diligently until she finds it? 9 And when she has found it, she calls together her friends and neighbors, saying, 'Rejoice with me, for I have found the coin which I had lost.' 10 Just so, I tell you, there is joy before the angels of God over one sinner who repents."

11 And he said, "There was a man who had two sons; 12 and the younger of them said to his father, 'Father, give me the share of property that falls to me.' And he divided his living between them. 13 Not many days later, the younger son gathered all he had and took his journey into a far country, and there he squandered his property in loose living. 14 And when he had spent everything, a great famine arose in that country, and he began to be in want. 15 So he went and joined himself to one of the citizens of that country, who sent him into his fields to feed swine. 16 And he would gladly have fed on the pods that the swine ate; and no one gave him anything. 17 But when he came to himself he said, 'How many of my father's hired servants have bread enough and to spare, but I perish here with hun-

ger! 18 I will arise and go to my father, and I will say to him, Father, I have sinned against heaven and before you; 19 I am no longer worthy to be called your son; treat me as one of your hired servants. ' 20 And he arose and came to his father. But while he was yet at a distance, his father saw him and had compassion, and ran and embraced him and kissed him. 21 And the son said to him, 'Father, I have sinned against heaven and before you; I am no longer worthy to be called your son.' 22 But the father said to his servants, 'Bring quickly the best robe, and put it on him; and put a ring on his hand, and shoes on his feet; 23 and bring the fatted calf and kill it, and let us eat and make merry; 24 for this my son was dead, and is alive again; he was lost, and is found.' And they began to make merry.

25 Now his elder son was in the field; and as he came and drew near to the house, he heard music and dancing. 26 And he called one of the servants and asked what this meant. 27 And he said to him, 'Your brother has come, and your father has killed the fatted calf, because he has received him safe and sound.' 28 But he was angry and refused to go in. His father came out and entreated him, 29 but he answered his father, 'Lo, these many years I have served you, and I never disobeyed your command; yet you never gave me a kid, that I might make merry with my friends. 30 But when this son of yours came, who has devoured your living with harlots, you killed for him the fatted calf!' 31 And he said to him, 'Son, you are always with me, all that is mine is yours. 32 It was fitting to make merry and be glad, for this your brother was dead, and is alive; he was lost, and is found.'"

The implication of the word "lost" should not be overlooked. To speak of something or someone as being "lost" is to say that that one is precious. A scrap of green paper carried by the wind into the gutter is not lost. But if that piece of paper is a $100 bill, we immediately say, it was obviously lost since it was precious to someone. In these parables Jesus is saying that all God's children — the thoughtless, the victimized, the willful, the smug, all of them, whatever their sin or their reason for disaffection and alienation — are precious to him and he wants them back in the family circle. This is the good news of the kingdom of God.

Foresight and Warning

Two parables deal with the question of wise foresight — present behaviour which casts a long shadow on one's future situation. The first is the story of a dishonest steward. Whether this manager of a rich man's estate was considered dishonest because of his former behavior (he is only charged with "wasting" his master's good), or because of what he now does is not clear. Nor is it clear whether the master of the estate commends him his sly dealings or whether "the master" is Jesus who is telling the parable to his disciples. In any case the point is that the steward looked ahead and patterned his present behavior with an eye to his future welfare. It is not likely that the story was original with Jesus. It is more likely that he is saying in effect, "This is the kind of thing which happens every day." He was not passing judgment on the morality of such dealings. He was not giving approval to sly, dishonest, under-cover practices. He *was* saying that the "sons of this world" think ahead and plan ahead. In that respect they are "wiser than the sons of light." If a dishonest worldling uses his money with an eye to his future well-being, how much more should an honest person use his own money to make friends so that "they (a euphemism for God) may receive you into the eternal habitations" (v. 9). This world offers us opportunities which are really tests of character. It is by our behavior in small matters that we show whether or not we are fit for larger responsibility. Worldly wealth is a trust — ours for a time — it does not really belong to us. But by the way we use it we show whether we are fit to be entrusted with the real wealth of the heavenly kingdom.

A miscellany of Jesus' sayings, some about money, some about other things, follows along after the Parable of the Dishonest Steward, like gulls following a fishing boat. Then comes another parable about using one's opportunities with foresight — the Parable of Dives and Lazarus.

The parable is the story of a rich man (Dives) and a poor man (Lazarus). In this world Dives enjoys his ease while Lazarus looks on in misery. In the next it is Lazarus' turn, and Dives looks on in misery. The story is not original with Jesus; probably it is Egyptian in origin. It is the way Jesus uses it that makes it distinctively his. The story is not, as one might suppose, about rewards and punishments — there is no suggestion that Lazarus was "good" and therefore got rewarded in the afterlife. Nor is Jesus giving us a peep at details of life beyond the grave. The story is about the kingdom of God. On the pleasant side, it says that evidence of the kingdom may be seen in the way people treat each other in this world. On the sterner side, it says that the judgment of the kingdom will certainly be a fact in the world to come. Dives uses his wealth selfishly and misses a kingdom opportunity here. In the hereafter he pleads ignorance and suggests that his brothers will not share his fate if they are forewarned. But he is told that even miracles will not convince those whose minds are closed to conviction. Jesus is saying, share in making the kingdom evident now or fall under the judgment of the kingdom in the hereafter — a parable of foresight and warning.

16:1–13

He also said to the disciples, "There was a rich man who had a steward, and charges were brought to him that this man was wasting his goods. 2 And he called him and said to him, 'What is this that I hear about you? Turn in the account of your stewardship, for you can no longer be steward.' 3 And the steward said to himself, 'What shall I do, since my master is taking the stewardship away from me? I am not strong enough to dig, and I am ashamed to beg. 4 I have decided what to do, so that people may receive me into their houses when I am put out of the stewardship.' 5 So, summoning his master's debtors one by one, he said to the first, 'How much do you owe my master?' He said, 'A hundred measures of oil.' And he said to him, 'Take your bill, and sit down quickly and write fifty.' 7 Then he said to another, 'And how much do you owe?' He said, 'A hundred measures of wheat.' He said to him, 'Take your bill, and write eighty.' 8 The master commended the dishonest steward for his shrewdness; for the sons of this world are more shrewd in dealing with their own generation than the sons of light. 9 And I tell you, make friends for yourselves by means of unrighteous mammon, so that when it fails they may receive you into the eternal habitations.

10 "He who is faithful in a very little is faithful also in much; and he who is dishonest in a very little is dishonest also in much. 11 If then you have not been faithful in the unrighteous mammon, who will entrust to you the true riches? 12 And if you have not been faithful in that which is another's, who will give you that which is your own? 13 No servant can serve two masters; for either he will hate the one and love the other, or he will be devoted to the one and despise the other. You cannot serve God and mammon." . . .

16:19–31

19 "There was a rich man, who was clothed in purple and fine linen and who feasted sumptuously every day. 20 And at his gate lay a poor man named Lazarus, full of sores, 21 who desired to be fed with what fell from the rich man's table; moreover the dogs came and licked his sores. 22 The poor man died and was carried by the angels to Abraham's bosom. The rich man also died and was buried; 23 and in Hades, being in torment, he lifted up his eyes, and saw Abraham far off and Lazarus

in his bosom. 24 And he called out, 'Father Abraham, have mercy upon me, and send Lazarus to dip the end of his finger in water and cool my tongue; for I am in anguish in this flame.' 25 But Abraham said, 'Son, remember that you in your lifetime received your good things, and Lazarus in like manner evil things; but now he is comforted here, and you are in anguish. 26 And besides all this, between us and you a great chasm has been fixed, in order that those who would pass from here to you may not be able, and none may cross from there to us.' 27 And he said, 'Then I beg you, father, to send him to my father's house, 28 for I have five brothers, so that he may warn them, lest they also come into this place of torment.' 29 But Abraham said, 'They have Moses and the prophets; let them hear them.' 30 And he said, 'No, father Abraham; but if some one goes to them from the dead, they will repent.' 31 He said to him, 'If they do not hear Moses and the prophets, neither will they be convinced if some one should rise from the dead.'"

The term "unrighteous mammon" is used for money. The point is that where there is money there is menace because money is the great rival of God for the devotion and service of men and women. One cannot serve God and money at the same time; that is what makes mammon "unrighteous." But to use money in doing good to others is to redeem it from its normally sinister character and exchange it for the currency of heaven.

Dives teaches us negatively a great deal about membership in the kingdom of God. In the hereafter he recognizes Lazarus, knows him by name ("that fellow who used to be out back by the garbage cans"), and continues to treat him as the second-rate citizen he had always thought of him as being: "Send Lazarus to my father's house . . . ," Lazarus the lackey. The attitudes we develop toward people and things in this world are carried with us into the hereafter. The qualities of life which make one a citizen of the kingdom of God are present traits, not future acquisitions.

The Coming of the Son of Man

In order to appreciate Jesus' words about the kingdom of God (whether thought of as "coming" or "in the midst of you") and about "the days of the Son of man," a little background is needed. These words have to do with eschatology, meaning beliefs about such final matters as the end of history and God's judgment at the end of time, or what is called "the last days." This subject is further complicated because catastrophic events within history are also thought of as God's judgment, and are considered a foretaste of what will one day come. In the last days Israel will be confronted with the ultimate issues of life and death, seeing clearly what is really important and what is trivial. So in Jesus Christ — what he says and does, and (because Luke was writing two generations later) his death and resurrection — these same life-and-death issues must now be faced. The Son of man image comes from the Book of Daniel (7:1, 9-28) in which this heavenly figure comes with the clouds of heaven, overthrows the pagan empires and establishes the kingdom of God forever. Jesus believes that he is to fulfill that destiny. His rejection by the religious leaders and his approaching death will bring on the coming of the kingdom which will happen as suddenly and unexpectedly as a lightning flash: there will be no warning signs. The people of Israel will be as unprepared for it as their ancestors were unprepared for catastrophe in the days of Noah and Lot. Nonetheless these things will take place as surely and as swiftly as vultures (more accurate than "eagles") gather round a camel that dies in the desert.

17:20-37

20 Being asked by the Pharisees when the kingdom of God was coming, he answered them, "The kingdom of God is not coming with signs to be observed; 21 nor will they say, 'Lo, here it is!' or 'There!' for behold, the kingdom of God is in the midst of you."

22 And he said to the disciples, "The days are coming when you will desire to see one of the days of the Son of man, and you will not see it. 23 And they will say to you,

'Lo, there!' or 'Lo, here!' Do not go, do not follow them. 24 For as the lightning flashes and lights up the sky from one side to the other, so will the Son of man be in his day. 25 But first he must suffer many things and be rejected by this generation. 26 As it was in the days of Noah, so will it be in the days of the Son of man. 27 They ate, they drank, they married, they were given in marriage, until the day when Noah entered the ark, and the flood came and destroyed them all. 28 Likewise as it was in the days of Lot — they ate, they drank, they bought, they sold, they planted, they built, 29 but on the day when Lot went out from Sodom fire and brimstone rained from heaven and destroyed them all — 30 so will it be on the day when the Son of man is revealed. 31 On that day, let him who is on the housetop, with his goods in the house, not come down to take them away; and likewise let him who is in the field not turn back. 32 Remember Lot's wife. 33 Whoever seeks to gain his life will lose it, but whoever loses his life will preserve it. 34 I tell you, in that night there will be two in one bed; one will be taken and the other left. 35 There will be two women grinding together; one will be taken and the other left."* 37 And they said to him, "Where, Lord?" He said to them, "Where the body is, there the eagles will be gathered together."

*Some ancient authorities add verse 36, *"Two men will be in the field; one will be taken and the other left."*

Because the Son is now "rejected," his second coming will be a time of judgment. There will be no time then to get prepared; one must already be prepared. The Pharisees are so obsessed with the idea that there would be a warning sign that they are going to fail to be ready. The disciples will fall into the same sign-wanting trap if they are not careful. (vs. 22).

Prayer

Luke now gives us two parables on prayer, a subject close to his heart which appears often in his gospel account. The closing comment of the first one indicates why these parables follow the section on the Last Days. When the Son of man comes he will surely vindicate those faithful ones who have persistently called to him. In the second, those who are found acceptable by God (and, of course, by the Son of man) are those who are honest about themselves and rely on divine mercy.

The Parable of the Unjust Judge strikes a note of reassurance. If an unscrupulous judge is finally swayed by the pleas of a persistent widow, how much more will persistence prevail with the Eternal Judge who is compassionate. The Parable of the Pharisee and the Tax Collector strikes a note of warning. The Pharisee does not really pray to God; he is busy patting himself on the back. If, when standing in God's presence, one is thinking of his own piety, he is putting a barrier between himself and God.

18:1–14

And he told them a parable, to the effect that they ought always to pray and not lose heart. 2 He said, "In a certain city there was a judge who neither feared God nor regarded man; 3 and there was a widow in that city who kept coming to him and saying, 'Vindicate me against my adversary.' 4 For a while he refused; but afterward he said to himself, 'Though I neither fear God nor regard man, 5 yet because this widow bothers me, I will vindicate her, or she will wear me out by her continual coming.'" 6 And the Lord said, "Hear what the unrighteous judge says. 7 And will not God vindicate his elect, who cry to him day and night? Will he delay long over them? 8 I tell you, he will vindicate them speedily. Nevertheless, when the Son of man comes, will he find faith on earth?"

9 He also told this parable to some who trusted in themselves that they were righteous and despised others: 10 "Two men went up into the temple to pray, one a Pharisee and the other a tax collector. 11 The Phari-

see stood and prayed thus with himself, 'God, I thank thee that I am not like other men, extortioners, unjust, adulterers, or even like this tax collector. 12 I fast twice a week, I give tithes of all that I get.' 13 But the tax collector, standing far off, would not even lift up his eyes to heaven, but beat his breast, saying, 'God, be merciful to me a sinner!' 14 I tell you, this man went down to his house justified rather than the other; for every one who exalts himself will be humbled, but he who humbles himself will be exalted."

"God's elect" (vs. 7) means, of course, God's favorite ones. This is misunderstood to mean that God elects some arbitrarily and rejects others—the favored and the damned. The Bible casts this matter in a different light. Israel became "God's elect" in the days of its humiliation—when they were slaves in Egypt. The prophets were always defending and Jesus was always reaching out to the poor, the sufferers, the persecuted—people especially favored by God because God has a bias toward innocent victims of persecution. This is what makes them "God's elect."

On Entering the Kingdom

Luke now deals in a Beethoven-like manner with the theme of the qualities one must have in order to enter the kingdom of God. In a Beethoven symphony one hears the melodic theme played by the strings, then the woodwinds, then the brass, and so on through the orchestra. Luke deals in a similar way with the qualities needed in order to enter the kingdom. First Jesus responds to the presence of infants, then to the questions of a rich ruler, then to Peter, and finally he sets the matter against the backdrop of what will shortly take place in Jerusalem.

18:15–34

15 Now they were bringing even infants to him that he might touch them; and when the disciples saw it, they rebuked them. 16 But Jesus called them to him, saying, "Let the children come to me, and do not hinder them; for to such belongs the kingdom of God.

17 Truly, I say to you, whoever does not receive the kingdom of God like a child shall not enter it."

18 And a ruler asked him, "Good Teacher, what shall I do to inherit eternal life?" 19 And Jesus said to him, "Why do you call me good? No one is good but God alone. 20 You know the commandments: Do not commit adultery, Do not kill, Do not steal, Do not bear false witness, Honor your father and mother." 21 And he said, "All these I have observed from my youth." 22 And when Jesus heard it, he said to him, "One thing you still lack. Sell all that you have and distribute to the poor, and you will have treasure in heaven; and come, follow me." 23 But when he heard this he became sad, for he was very rich. 24 Jesus looking at him said, "How hard it is for those who have riches to enter the kingdom of God! 25 For it is easier for a camel to go through the eye of a needle than for a rich man to enter the kingdom of God." 26 Those who heard it said, "Then who can be saved?" 27 But he said, "What is impossible with men is possible with God." 28 And Peter said, "Lo, we have left our homes and followed you." 29 And he said to them, "Truly, I say to you, there is no man who has left house or wife or brothers or parents or children, for the sake of the kingdom of God, 30 who will not receive manifold more in this time, and in the age to come eternal life."

31 And taking the twelve, he said to them, "Behold, we are going up to Jerusalem, and everything that is written of the Son of man by the prophets will be accomplished. 32 For he will be delivered to the Gentiles, and will be mocked and shamefully treated and spit upon; 33 they will scourge him and kill him, and on the third day he will rise." 34 But they understood none of these things; this saying was hid from them, and they did not grasp what was said.

Adults are inclined to think of becoming a disciple and entering God's kingdom as the result of something they *do*. Certainly the Pharisee in the Parable of the Pharisee and the Tax Collector thought of his goodness as an accomplishment (18:9-14). Jesus has an entirely different view. When mothers bring their infants for him to bless (it was common practice to bring one's baby to a rabbi for his blessing), he used the occasion to explain that infants have innately that wonderful trait one needs to enter the kingdom: receptivity. Little children are not proudly self-sufficient; they can accept what is given without embarrassment, indeed, they delight in receiving presents. The key word is "receive" — "*receive* the kingdom of God like a child"; one cannot *do* anything to deserve to enter the kingdom. It is God's gift.

Then a well-to-do official comes to Jesus: "What shall I *do* to enter God's kingdom?" (That is what "inherit eternal life" means.) He was in the habit of "doing"; he was a man in control. If what was required was morality, he qualified, he was on top of the situation, he kept the Commandments. If something else was required, because of his wealth, possessions, education, influential connections, he could produce. "No," Jesus says. "Get out of the driver's seat. Give away all your control and power, and come follow me." Discipleship means accepting Jesus as Lord . . . of ALL. What Jesus was implying earlier when he spoke of "unrighteous mammon" (16:1-12) he now makes more explicit. Truly, money *is* God's rival. It makes us think we, rather than God, are in control of life.

Peter's reaction to Jesus' words leads the Master to say that self-denial for the sake of the kingdom will be vindicated. And then the Lord again predicts what will happen when they reach Jerusalem. He has specifically predicted his passion twice before (9:22 and 44), and has alluded to it several times (12:50; 13:32; 17:25). Here side by side are the responses of people to the gospel of the kingdom and the foreshadowing of the events which will take place in Jersualem. Luke is setting the promise of eternal life and Lord's sacrifice in juxtaposition. The Lord's passion will replace human self-sufficiency with the all-sufficiency of divine love. But the disciples do not understand what their Scriptures foretold about the Messiah, and they will not understand until their Lord has risen from the dead (24:13-32).

The Rejected King

On the last leg of the "journey" of Jesus and his disciples to Jerusalem they become part of a large company of pilgrims en route to the Holy City to celebrate the Feast of the Passover. The multitude is excited to have Jesus in their midst and this excitement becomes even greater when Jesus heals a blind roadside beggar. The fellow's persistent cry, "Jesus, Son of David, have mercy on me," was only partially shushed by those near him ("Shut up! How can I hear Jesus when you are making such a fuss?"). Actually, the man's words caused the strings of hope to reverberate in the hearts of many a devout pilgrim. Would not the messianic king, the Son of David, free them from the Romans? That beggar did not invent the title, he had heard it on the lips of many a passerby that day and earlier. Moreover, when Jesus healed him, this caused an added ripple of excited comments. Had not the prophets repeatedly foretold that the Suffering Servant of God would open the eyes of the blind? (Isa. 29:18; 35:5; 42:7) No wonder the people glorified God. No wonder they supposed the kingdom would appear immediately.

While Jesus is passing through Jericho another incident of persistent faith occurs. Zacchaeus was "a chief tax collector." This meant that he had bought the local taxing rights from the Roman government, and he could therefore set the tax amount at will from which he paid the Romans a contracted amount. Quite obviously, he was detested by his fellow countrymen and socially ostracized. He was by definition a crook, getting rich at the expense of his own people. Because of his unpopularity, it was dangerous for him to venture into a crowd. For him to want to see Jesus badly enough to take that risk and even climb a tree where all could see him took courage and determination; he might have been lynched. The qualities of a true disciple — faith and persistence — are demonstrated by Zacchaeus as they had been by the blind beggar.

The Parable of the Pounds is complicated by the fact that two stories have been telescoped—a story of a rejected king (vss. 12, 14, 27) and a parable about the meaning of discipleship (vss. 13, 15-26).

18:35-43

35 As he drew near to Jericho, a blind man was sitting by the roadside begging; 36 and hearing a multitide going by, he inquired what this meant. 37 They told him, "Jesus of Nazareth is passing by." 38 And he cried, "Jesus, Son of David, have mercy on me!" 39 And those who were in front rebuked him, telling him to be silent; but he cried out all the more, "Son of David, have mercy of me!" 40 And Jesus stopped, and commanded him to be brought to him; and when he came near, he asked him, 41 "What do you want me to do for you?" He said, "Lord, let me receive my sight." 42 And Jesus said to him, "Receive your sight; your faith has made you well." 43 And immediately he received his sight and followed him, glorifying God; and all the people, when they saw it, gave praise to God.

19:1-28

He entered Jericho and was passing through. 2 And there was a man named Zacchaeus; he was a chief tax collector, and rich. 3 And he sought to see who Jesus was, but could not, on account of the crowd, because he was small of stature. 4 So he ran on ahead and climbed up into a sycamore tree to see him, for he was to pass that way. 5 And when Jesus came to the place, he looked up and said to him, "Zacchaeus, make haste and come down; for I must stay at your house today." 6 So he made haste and came down, and received him joyfully. 7 And when they saw it they all murmured, "He has gone in to be the guest of a man who is a sinner." 8 And Zacchaeus stood and said to the Lord,

"Behold, Lord, the half of my goods I give to the poor; and if I have defrauded any one of anything, I restore it fourfold." 9 And Jesus said to him, "Today salvation has come to this house, since he also is a son of Abraham. 10 For the Son of man came to seek and to save the lost."

11 As they heard these things, he proceeded to tell a parable, because he was near to Jerusalem, and because they supposed that the kingdom of God was to appear immediately. 12 He said therefore, "A nobleman went into a far country to receive a kingdom and then return. 13 Calling ten of his servants, he gave them ten pounds, and said to them, 'Trade with these till I come.' 14 But his citizens hated him and sent an embassy after him, saying, 'We do not want this man to reign over us.' 15 When he returned, having received the kingdom, he commanded these servants, to whom he had given the money, to be called to him, that he might know what they had gained by trading. 16 The first came before him, saying, 'Lord, your pound has made ten pounds more.' 17 And he said to him, 'Well done, good servant! Because you have been faithful in a very little, you shall have authority over ten cities.' 18 And the second came, saying, 'Lord, your pound has made five pounds.' 19 And he said to him, 'And you are to be over five cities.' 20 Then another came, saying, 'Lord, here is your pound, which I kept laid away in a napkin; 21 for I was afraid of you, because you are a severe man; you take up what you did not lay down, and reap what you did not sow.' 22 He said to him, 'I will condemn you out of your own mouth, you wicked servant! You knew that I was a severe man, taking up what I did not lay down and reaping what I did not sow? 23 Why then did you not put my money into the bank, and at my coming I should have collected it with interest?' 24 And he said to those who stood by, 'Take

the pound from him, and give it to him who has the ten pounds.' 25 (And they said to him, 'Lord, he has ten pounds!') 26 'I tell you, that to every one who has will more be given; but from him who has not, even what he has will be taken away. 27 But as for these enemies of mine, who did not want me to reign over them, bring them here and slay them before me.'"

28 And when he had said this, he went on ahead, going up to Jerusalem.

The Parable of the Pounds with its rejected-king overlay has a carefully planned place as the concluding piece in the "journey" section of this Gospel. What had just happened fired people's yearning for the coming kingdom — the healing of the blind beggar with all of its messianic overtones, and the way Jesus, the messianic shepherd, reaches out to and embraces Zacchaeus, symbol of all outcasts because he is so unlikely a candidate for salvation. No wonder people thought "the kingdom of God was to appear immediately" (19:11). Indeed, an expectation of the last days and the coming kingdom was widespread in the Church during the years following the Lord's death, resurrection, and ascension. In addressing the people within the gospel story Luke is also addressing the members of the Church of his own day. The parable, which is part allegory, says in effect: "No, the Risen Lord's return will not be immediate. He goes to heaven and receives his appointment as messianic king. The Jews hate him and do not wish him to rule over them. In his absence Christians are entrusted with responsibilities. On his return he will reward his servants according to their diligence and will punish his enemies."

A principal theme of the teaching material in the "journey" section has had to do with the meaning of discipleship. The focal point now shifts from the disciple to the Lord, from the servant to "the Son of David," the Rejected King and his coming passion.

CHAPTER 6

JERUSALEM: PREDICTIONS
AND ARGUMENTS

Jesus plans a demonstration for his arrival in Jerusalem. By his teaching and actions he has been showing that the kingdom of God is a present reality, and it is becoming increasingly obvious to his followers that he is the Messianic King. Now he is coming to "the city of the great King" (Ps. 48). General messianic expectation was that the king would head a revolt to drive the Romans out. This was especially true at Passover time when the Messiah was supposed to appear. Jesus wants to allay rather than arouse this national fervor. He wants to make clear exactly the kind of king he intends to be. Prophetic words in Zechariah 9:9-10 are the model for his demonstration: he will be a humble king of peace riding upon a lowly donkey, rather than a warrior king on his prancing battle steed. His disciples sing of God's gift of peace which has been prepared in heaven. The scene is warm as sunshine. But the Pharisees, fearful that this outburst of enthusiasm may be interpreted by the Romans as seditious and thus bring on reprisals, caution Jesus to quell this enthusiasm. He replies in effect that all of Israel's history has been a preparation for this moment — the coming of the Messiah to the Holy City — and that if people do not recognize that fact and shout, the very stones underfoot will chorus his coming.

But Jerusalem is not ready to receive him. Jericho's blind man had recognized him, but the leaders in Jerusalem, so intent on their own power and prestige, cannot see that their Savior has come. Hence his coming both now and at the end of the age will be for them judgment rather than salvation.

When the Messianic King arrives in his city he immediately goes and takes possession of "my house," the Temple. Jewish law required that pilgrims' offerings must be in Jewish currency, not Roman, and that the animal or bird they brought for sacrifice be "without blemish" (Lev. 1:3). This is the reason for the market in the court of the Gentiles—moneychanging and the inspecting or selling of a proper sacrifice. But how can the faith of Israel be "a light for revelation to the Gentiles" (2:32) if the court of the Gentiles is a yammering arena of hucksters? Jesus takes possession: he drives out the peddlers. This high-handed action in the Temple further alienates the religious authorities and steels their determination to find a way to get rid of him.

19:29-48

29 When he drew near to Bethphage and Bethany, at the mount that is called Olivet, he sent two of his disciples, 30 saying, "Go into the village opposite,where on entering you will find a colt tied, on which no one has ever yet sat; untie it and bring it here. 31 If any one asks you, 'Why are you untying it?' you shall say this, 'The Lord has need of it.'" 32 So those who were sent went away and found it as he had told them. 33 And as they were untying the colt, its owners said to them, "Why are you untying the colt?" 34 And they said, "The Lord has need of it." 35 And they brought it to Jesus, and throwing their garments on the colt they set Jesus upon it. 36 And as he rode along, they spread their garments on the road. 37 As he was now drawing near, at the descent of the Mount of Olives, the whole multitude of the disciples began to rejoice and praise God with a loud voice for all the mighty works that they had seen, 38 saying,
"Blessed is the King who comes in the name of the Lord! Peace in heaven and glory in the highest!"

39 And some of the Pharisees in the multitude said to him, "Teacher, rebuke your disciples." 40 He answered, "I tell you, if these were silent, the very stones would cry out."

41 And when he drew near and saw the city he wept over it, 42 saying, "Would that even today you knew the things that make for peace! But now they are hid from your eyes. 43 For the days shall come upon you, when your enemies will cast up a bank about you and surround you, and hem you in on every side, 44 and dash you to the ground, you and your children within you, and they will not leave one stone upon another in you; because you did not know the time of your visitation."

45 And he entered the temple and began to drive out those who sold, 46 saying to them, "It is written, 'My house shall be a house of prayer'; but you have made it a den of robbers."

47 And he was teaching daily in the temple. The chief priests and the scribes and the principal men of the people sought to destroy him; 48 but they did not find anything they could do, for all the people hung upon his words.

As we have seen earlier, Luke uses a transition piece to carry his readers from one phase of his story to the next (as we saw 2:41-52 and 4:16-30 were used in this way). The Lord's coming to Jerusalem, weeping over it, and cleansing the Temple serve that purpose here. Just before Jesus' birth Zechariah sang:

Blessed be the Lord God of Israel,

For he has visited and redeemed his people. (1:68)

But "his people" in the persons of their leaders reject him, hence his tears over the Jerusalem he loves.

This is the last time Luke speaks of Jesus' opponents as "the Pharisees." After this they are referred to as "the chief priests and the scribes and the principal men of the people" who seek a way to destroy him. These persons comprise the Sanhedrin, the highest governing body of the Jews, official Israel. And in cleansing the Temple Jesus has just given many of them an additional reason to hate him, for the chief priests benefited from the profits of the Temple market which Jesus had disrupted. The whole focus now is on the mortal struggle between Jesus, the Messianic King, and the Sanhedrin whose members are fiercely determined to protect their authority and their bank accounts.

The Temple Debate

Several confrontations now take place between Jesus and members of the Sanhedrin, the latter being like a sparring boxer who is looking for a hole in his opponent's defense. Their first jab is to question Jesus' authority in taking such high-handed action in the Temple. He has not gone through proper channels for authorization.

20:1-8

> One day, as he was teaching the people in the temple and preaching the gospel, the chief priests and the scribes with the elders came up 2 and said to him, "Tell us by what authority you do these things, or who it is that gave you this authority." 3 He answered them, "I also will ask you a question; now tell me, 4 Was the baptism of John from heaven or from men?" 5 And they discussed it with one another, saying, "If we say, 'From heaven,' he will say, 'Why did you not believe him?' 6 But if we say, 'From men,' all the people will stone us; for they are convinced that John was a prophet." 7 So they answered that they did not know whence it was. 8 And Jesus said to them, "Neither will I tell you by what authority I do these things."

They lose that first round; Jesus turns the question back on them and puts them on the defensive. But he does not stop there, rather he goes on to tell his hearers the Parable of the Wicked Tenants in which it is obvious to the religious authorities "that he had told this parable against them" (v. 19). The tenants en trusted with God's vineyard (Israel) had proven unworthy of their trust, even to the point of killing God's Son. The people are shocked; the leaders are furious, and redouble their efforts to trap him.

20:9-19

9 And he began to tell the people this parable: "A man planted a vineyard, and let it out to tenants, and went into another country for a long while. 10 When the time came, he sent a servant to the tenants, that they should give him some of the fruit of the vineyard; but the tenants beat him, and sent him away empty-handed . 11 And he sent another servant; him also they beat and treated shamefully, and sent him away empty-handed. 12 And he sent yet a third; this one they wounded and cast out. 13 Then the owner of the vineyard said, 'What shall I do? I will send my beloved son; it may be they will respect him.' 14 But when the tenants saw him, they said to themselves, 'This is the heir; let us kill him, that the inheritance may be ours.' 15 And they cast him out of the vineyard and killed him. What then will the owner of the vineyard do to them? 16 He will come and destroy those tenants, and give the vineyard to others." When they heard this, they said, "God forbid!" 17 But he looked at them and said, "What then is this that is written:
'The very stone which the builders rejected
has become the head of the corner'?
18 Every one who falls on that stone will be broken to pieces; but when it falls on any one it will crush him."
19 The scribes and the chief priests tried to lay hands on him at that very hour, but they feared the people; for they perceived that he had told this parable against them.

The authorities now change their tactics. Instead of attacking Jesus directly they send well-coached spies who pretend to be friends from the multitude of his followers. They ask a political question about paying taxes, those unpopular Roman taxes. Either way he answers they are sure they have him. If he favors the tax, he will lose his popular following; if he opposes paying it, the Romans will arrest him.

20:20-26

> 20 So they watched him, and sent spies, who pretended to be sincere, that they might take hold of what he said, so as to deliver him up to the authority and jurisdiction of the governor. 21 They asked him, "Teacher, we know that you speak and teach rightly, and show no partiality, but truly teach the way of God. 22 Is it lawful for us to give tribute to Caesar, or not?" 23 But he perceived their craftiness, and said to them, 24 "Show me a coin. Whose likeness and inscription has it?" They said, "Caesar's." 25 He said to them, "Then render to Caesar the things that are Caesar's, and to God the things that are God's." 26 And they were not able in the presence of the people to catch him by what he said; but marveling at his answer they were silent.

Jesus' answer makes it clear that as part of our historic existence we are subjected to both an earthly and a heavenly kingdom. To each we owe loyalty — to God, it is absolute; to the State, it is conditional, that is, so long as Caesar performs his God-given role of providing a framework of order for the common life of man. No one had ever made this distinction so clear before. They marvel at his insight and are silenced. There is a certain awesome magic in the beauty of revealed truth which silences prattle. In the presence of Leonardo da Vinci's "Mona Lisa" or Michelangelo's "Pietà" a chattering crowd of sightseers becomes subdued. So here. The beautiful clarity of Jesus' grasp of truth momentarily silences his enemies.

The Question of the Resurrection

The members of the Sanhedrin were of two major religious points of view. The Sadducees were the conservatives; only the Pentateuch (the first five books of the Old Testament) was considered the source of the Law and its meaning. The resurrection of the dead is not mentioned in those books so the Sadducees do not believe in it — body and soul are mortal and both cease to exist at death. The Pharisees and their scribes take a broader view. The rest of what we call the Old Testament throws light on the meaning of the Pentatuech, and as a result they do believe in the resurrection of the dead (see Isa. 26:19 and Dan. 12:2).

The Sadducees' mocking question to Jesus presents resurrection belief as an absurdity. Jesus answers them in their own terms; he plays their game, so to speak. The earthly reason for marriage is to propagate the race. Since those in heaven will not die, propagation (and therefore marriage) is unnecessary. The scribes of the Pharisees are pleased with his answer.

20:27–40

> 27 There came to him some Sadducees, those who say that there is no resurrection, 28 and they asked him a question saying, "Teacher, Moses wrote for us that if a man's brother dies, having a wife but no children, the man must take the wife and raise up children for his brother. 29 Now there were seven brothers; the first took a wife, and died without children; 30 and the second 31 and the third took her, and likewise all seven left no children and died. 32 Afterward the woman also died. 33 In the resurrection, therefore, whose wife will the woman be? For the seven had her as wife."
>
> 34 And Jesus said to them, "The sons of this age marry and are given in marriage; 35 but those who are accounted worthy to attain to that age and to the resurrection from the dead neither marry nor are given in marriage, 36 for they cannot die any more, because they are equal to angels and are sons of God, being sons

of the resurrection. 37 But that the dead are raised, even Moses showed, in the passage about the bush, where he calls the Lord the God of Abraham and the God of Isaac and the God of Jacob. 38 Now he is not God of the dead, but of the living; for all live to him." 39 And some of the scribes answered, "Teacher, you have spoken well." 40 For they no longer dared to ask him any question.

In each instance Jesus takes the question more seriously than does the person asking it. On the question of authority, instead of bickering over bureaucratic details of proper permission to act, Jesus embarrasses those members of the Sanhedrin because they had not taken John the Baptist seriously and formed an opinion about him. Consequently, they were not prepared to receive the Messiah. His Parable of the Wicked Tenants showed the result of that failure. On the question of paying the tax, he raised their sights from the performance of an irritating civil duty to their loyal duty to God. On the question of the resurrection of the dead, he turned an in-house theological debate into a vision of friendship with God — Abraham was a friend of God here on earth and it was incredible that such friendship should end at death.

Of David's Son

Jesus now becomes the questioner. The common view of the Son-of-David Messiah was that he would be a militant, warrior king who would sweep all before him — Roman oppressors, lawless Gentiles, sinners. No, said Jesus. He, the true Messiah, was more than just a lineal descendant of David, he was also David's Lord.

This section of arguments and questions closes with Jesus' condemnation of the hypocritical piety of the religious leaders. Jesus is speaking in the context of his mission, but Luke is writing at the time of the developing mission of the Christian Church. Luke's Gospel was certainly intended to be read *in* Church; it is conceivable that he thought of it as being read *to* the Church and her leaders. That would give it a special relevance. That would also put the widow's example of true piety not only over against the comfortable religiosity of the rich of Jesus' day, but also as a beacon of true piety. For such noble souls the coming kingdom will bring deliverance from oppression and also fulfillment of their hope in God.

20:41-47

> 41 But he said to them, "How can they say that the Christ is David's son? 42 For David himself says in the Book of the Psalms,
>> 'The Lord said to my Lord,
>> Sit at my right hand,
>> till I make thy enemies a stool for thy feet.'
> 44 David thus calls him Lord; so how is he his son?"
> 45 And in the hearing of all the people he said to his disciples, 46 "Beware of the scribes, who like to go about in long robes, and love salutations in the market places and the best seats in the synagogues and the places of honor at feasts, 47 who devour widows' houses and for a pretence make long prayers. They will receive the greater condemnation."

21:1-4

> He looked up and saw the rich putting their gifts into the treasury; 2 and he saw a poor widow put in two copper coins. 3 And he said, "Truly I tell you, this poor widow has put in more than all of them; 4 for they all contributed out of their abundance, but she out of her poverty put in all the living that she had."

The Coming Difficult Times

The coming of the Messiah meant that Israel's redemption had come. But for official Israel, which rejected Jesus the Messiah and was shortly to do its uttermost to destroy him, that coming was a day of judgment. This is spelled out in an apocalyptic passage about the signs of the times and the end of the age (21:5-38). (See the discussion of "the days of the Son of Man," page 107.) This topic has been the subject of more scholarly debate than any other passage in the Gospels. Let others detail the various scholarly views and conclusions. Here we will only attempt to help the reader have some intelligent appreciation of the passage.

Jesus' journey has taken him to Jerusalem. He enters and laments over the city which will reject him. Then, anticipating Israel's consequent fate, he pronounces solemn judgment. Appreciation of the passage is complicated by the fact that Luke is writing several decades after the crucifixion-resurrection and not very long after the Romans had destroyed Jerusalem. Scholars disagree about the meaning of judgment; what is the connection between the destruction of Jerusalem and the foretold end of the world? They also differ about how much of Luke's account was said by Jesus before the crucifixion and how much of it was by (or addressed to) members of the early Church.

The crucial question here is about the coming day of judgment. The disciples ask Jesus: "Teacher, when will this be, and what will be the sign when this is about to take place?" (v. 7). As Jesus had repeatedly warned his disciples throughout his ministry, the time was coming when he, their Lord, would be taken away (5:35; 12:35-48) and they would experience difficult days. They would long for his return, but were warned not to be misled by false announcers of his coming. They would be persecuted, but must endure. The passage reads like a pep talk to a beleaguered Church.

21:5-19

5 And as some spoke of the temple, how it was adorned with noble stones and offerings, he said, 6 "As for these things which you see, the days will come when there shall not be left here one stone upon another that will not be thrown down." 7 And they asked him,

"Teacher, when will this be, and what will be the sign when this is about to take place?" 8 And he said, "Take heed that you are not led astray; for many will come in my name, saying, 'I am he!' and, 'The time is at hand!' Do not go after them. 9 And when you hear of wars and tumults, do not be terrified; for this must first take place, but the end will not be at once."

10 Then he said to them, "Nation will rise against nation, and kingdom against kingdom; 11 there will be great earthquakes, and in various places famines and pestilences; and there will be terrors and great signs from heaven. 12 But before all this they will lay their hands on you and persecute you, delivering you up to the synagogues and prisons, and you will be brought before kings and governors for my name's sake. 13 This will be a time for you to bear testimony. 14 Settle it therefore in your minds, not to meditate beforehand how to answer; 15 for I will give you a mouth and wisdom, which none of your adversaries will be able to withstand or contradict. 16 You will be delivered up even by parents and brothers and kinsmen and friends, and some of you they will put to death; 17 you will be hated by all for my name's sake. 18 But not a hair of your head will perish. 19 By your endurance you will gain your lives."

The Times of the Gentile

Then will follow politically crushing circumstances (perhaps Luke had the fall of Jerusalem in mind), but this is not to be confused with the final crisis of history. These will be "the times of the Gentiles" (v.24) who like Cyrus of old (Isa. 45:1-4) will be instruments of the "days of vengeance" (v. 22). This does not refer to the wrath of a vengeful God, but rather to the result when sin has gone long unchecked and is inexorably confronted with the punishing justice of God.

To the Jews there were angelic beings appointed by God to rule over the destinies of pagan nations (Isa. 24:21; 34:1-4). These are "the powers of the heavens" which will be unseated in the "days of vengeance." The passage is not describing a cosmic cataclysm; rather it is to be taken figuratively.

21:20-28

> 20 "But when you see Jerusalem surrounded by armies, then know that its desolation has come near. 21 Then let those who are in Judea flee to the mountains, and let those who are inside the city depart, and let not those who are out in the country enter it; 22 for these are days of vengeance, to fulfill all that is written. 23 Alas for those who are with child and for those who give suck in those days! For great distress shall be upon the earth and wrath upon this people; 24 they will fall by the edge of the sword, and be led captive among all nations; and Jerusalem will be trodden down by the Gentiles, until the times of the Gentiles are fulfilled.
>
> 25 "And there will be signs in sun and moon and stars, and upon the earth distress of nations in perplexity at the roaring of the sea and the waves, 26 men fainting with fear and with foreboding of what is coming on the world; for the powers of the heavens will be shaken. 27 And then they will see the Son of man coming in a cloud with power and great glory. 28 Now when these things begin to take place, look up and raise your heads, because your redemption is drawing near."

The Coming of the Kingdom

The question is, When, when will evil be vanquished? The answer is not definite. (Mark thought it would be during his generation, Mk. 13:30.) For Luke the time of the final Day of Judgment is indefinite: "The end will not be at once," said Jesus (v. 9), and "the kingdom of God is near" (v. 31). The time of Jesus will be followed by the time of the Church for an indefinite future. It will be a time of testing, of witness, and of preparation for that final Day of the Lord. Persecution and the siege of Jerusalem will be the experience of "this generation." The disciples are both fore-warned and urged to be prepared. "Watch at all times, praying that you will have strength to escape all these things that will take place, and to stand before the Son of man" (22:36).

21:29–38

29 And he told them a parable: "Look at the fig tree, and all the trees; 30 as soon as they come out in leaf, you see for yourselves and know that the summer is already near. 31 So also, when you see these things taking place, you know that the kingdom of God is near. 32 Truly, I say to you, this generation will not pass away till all has taken place. 33 Heaven and earth will pass away, but my words will not pass away.

34 "But take heed to yourselves lest your hearts be weighed down with dissipation and drunkenness and cares of this life, and that day come upon you suddenly like a snare; 35 for it will come upon all who dwell upon the face of the whole earth. 36 But watch at all times, praying that you may have strength to escape all these things that will take place, and to stand before the Son of man."

37 And every day he was teaching in the temple, but at night he went out and lodged on the mount called Olivet. 38 And early in the morning all the people came to him in the temple to hear him.

The Jerusalem days of teaching begin in the Temple and end in the Temple (19:45, 47; 21:37-38). And while the Temple authorities desperately wanted to get rid of Jesus, they could not. The throngs of people who daily came to hear him had built a hedge of hearty approval about him that the religious leaders could not penetrate.

CHAPTER 7

THE LAST SUPPER

The seven days of the Feast of Unleavened Bread were at hand and the Passover was the first day of that feast. Jerusalem was crowded with pilgrims and among them was Jesus whom the members of the Sanhedrin were determined to get rid of because his volcanic teachings were damaging their reputation and authority. Would the people follow him, perhaps in a revolt? Certainly they would resent and perhaps resist his public arrest. Then the authorities got a break: Judas came to them with a proposition.

Why did he do it? Judas' reasons for betraying Jesus have fascinated many. Luke's own answer is simple: "Satan entered into Judas." Jesus and the early Church were conscious of a cosmic struggle going on between the powers of heaven and the powers of darkness, between Jesus the Messiah and Satan. Jesus had defeated the Tempter when he tried to subvert his motives and his mission in the wilderness (4:1-13). During Jesus' ministry God's purposes were being fulfilled and Satan could not gain a foothold. But now Judas gives him his first opportunity since those wilderness days of long ago. (See page 27.)

While Judas is engaged in his nefarious arrangements with the religious authorities, Peter and John are, at Jesus' direction, making the necessary preparations for all of them to eat their Passover meal in the Holy City. The time arrives, and Jesus and The Twelve gather in that upper room for their last supper together.

(One New Testament scholar has called Luke's account of the

Last Supper "a scholar's paradise and a beginner's nightmare." There are many problems about what was the original text, and many differences of opinion about how Luke handled the material he had in hand and exactly what was being celebrated. There is a jumble of conflicting theories about all of these matters which would take thousands of words to unravel. We, however, can be appreciative readers of the text before us without full knowledge of all the scholarly details of textual criticism. So we shall by-pass but not distort those technical questions.)

In Luke's account of what takes place at that meal, Jesus gives the disciples first the cup, then the bread, and then the cup a second time. There probably were variations among early Christians as to the way they observed the Lord's Supper. (I Corinthians 10:16,21 certainly suggests that worshippers received the cup before the bread.) Luke's account may have been one basis for such differences or, after the fact, may have reflected some of that lack of uniformity. However, the oldest New Testament account of the Last Supper is that of Paul (I Cor. 11:23-27) — bread first and then the cup — and the wording there is similar to the words used in celebrating the Lord's Supper in most present-day churches.

The supper has a two-fold significance which came about because it was related to the Passover meal on the one hand, and inexorably associated with Jesus' death on the other. So perhaps from the very first the regular celebration of this meal included both commemoration of the Lord's passion and anticipation of the heavenly banquet in the kingdom of God.

22:1–23

Now the feast of Unleavened Bread drew near, which is called the Passover. 2 And the chief priests and the scribes were seeking how to put him to death; for they feared the people.

3 Then Satan entered into Judas called Iscariot, who

was of the number of the twelve; 4 he went away and conferred with the chief priests and officers how he might betray him to them. 5 And they were glad, and engaged to give him money. 6 So he agreed, and sought an opportunity to betray him to them in the absence of the multitude.

7 Then came the day of Unleavened Bread, on which the passover lamb had to be sacrificed. 8 So Jesus sent Peter and John, saying, "Go and prepare the passover for us, that we may eat it." 9 They said to him, "Where will you have us prepare it?" 10 He said to them, "Behold, when you have entered the city, a man carrying a jar of water will meet you; follow him into the house which he enters, 11 and tell the householder, 'The Teacher says to you, Where is the guest room, where I am to eat the passover with my disciples?' 12 And he will show you a large upper room furnished; there make ready." 13 And they went, and found it as he had told them; and they prepared the passover.

14 And when the hour came, he sat at table, and the apostles with him. 15 And he said to them, "I have earnestly desired to eat this passover with you before I suffer; 16 for I tell you I shall not eat it until it is fulfilled in the kingdom of God." 17 And he took a cup, and when he had given thanks he said, "Take this, and divide it among yourselves; 18 for I tell you that from now on I shall not drink of the fruit of the vine until the kingdom of God comes." 19 And he took bread, and when he had given thanks he broke it and gave it to them, saying, "This is my body which is given for you. Do this in remembrance of me." 20 And likewise the cup after supper, saying, "This cup which is poured out for you is the new covenant in my blood. 21 But behold the hand of him who betrays me is with me on the table. 22 For the Son of man goes as it has been determined; but woe to that man by whom he is betrayed!" 23 And they began

to question one another, which of them it was that
would do this.

Jesus and his disciples were celebrating the Passover. (Matthew
and Mark agree; in John it is a pre-Passover meal, Jn. 18:28;
19:14.) That feast-meal commemorated the deliverance of the Is-
raelites from Egypt long ago and it anticipated the coming messianic deliverance. The blood of a lamb had saved their forebears
from death at the time of the first Passover (Exod. 12:7-13). So
the blood of Jesus was to bring into being a new covenant and ini-
tiate a new exodus, a freeing from the slavery of sin and death.

Upper Room Discourse

Now we come to Jesus' final talk with his disciples and it is filled
with pathos. Discipleship is the theme — theirs and his. The subject is kicked off by the disciples' littleness: "I'm more important
than you." Pagan, worldly values are not kingdom values, Jesus
tells them. Beware of equating greatness with power and dignity
with recognition. In the kingdom greatness and recognition go to
those who give of themselves in humble service. Jesus points to his
own ministry to illustrate his meaning: "I am among you as one
who serves."

For him, the life of service had brought on a series of trials —
tests of spiritual stamina. The temptations in the wilderness
showed Jesus choosing the way of humble service rather than that
of supremacy and headship. His ministry was a continual reaching down to help, expressions of self-giving love for others. Because of the adoring crowds there was always the temptation to
accept some sort of worldly lordship. In John's Gospel the people
actually try "to take him by force and make him king" (Jn.
6:14-15). Jesus called all this "my trials," and he appreciated the
companionship of his chosen disciples during all of that time.
The final wrestling was yet to come in the Garden of Gethsemane, but he appreciated their loyalty to this point.

Ultimately their loyalty would be rewarded. In "my kingdom"
they would "judge the twelve tribes of Israel," meaning have au-

thority, but only such authority as belongs to those who on earth have learned the meaning of service. The Twelve were to be the nucleus of the New Israel. The Old Israel by rejecting the Messiah had lost its birthright. However, when his final testing came the disciples would fall away. The Lord's prediction is not clear in English. Here is a more literal translation of the Greek text:

Simon, Simon, behold, Satan demanded to have all of you, that he might sift you like wheat, but I have prayed for you, Simon, that your faith may not fail; and when you have turned again, strengthen your brethren. (22:31-32)

Simon Peter had always been the leader of The Twelve and would continue to be in time to come.

The final interchange shows how far the disciples are from understanding their Lord. Jesus recalls the balmy days when he first sent them out on their own. Then with the kind of exaggerated figure of speech he liked to use he says in effect, "Things will be difficult. You'll need a sword more than a coat." Taking him literally they miss the point: "Lord, here are two swords." He gives up; they are so far from appreciating his meaning. "That's enough of that," he says, and with that their evening ends.

22:24-38

24 A dispute also arose among them, which of them was to be regarded as the greatest. 25 And he said to them, "The kings of the Gentiles exercise lordship over them; and those in authority over them are called benefactors. 26 But not so with you; rather let the greatest among you become as the youngest, and the leader as one who serves. 27 For which is the greater, one who sits at table, or one who serves? Is it not the one who sits at table? But I am among you as one who serves.

28 "You are those who have continued with me in my trials; 29 and I assign to you, as my Father assigned to me, a kingdom, 30 that you may eat and drink at my table in my kingdom, and sit on thrones judging the twelve tribes of Israel.

31 "Simon, Simon, behold, Satan demanded to have you, that he might sift you like wheat, 32 but I have prayed for you that your faith may not fail; and when you have turned again, strengthen your brethren." 33 And he said to him, "Lord, I am ready to go with you to prison and to death." 34 He said, "I tell you, Peter, the cock will not crow this day, until you three times deny that you know me."

35 And he said to them, "When I sent you out with no purse or bag or sandals, did you lack anything?" They said, "Nothing." 36 He said to them, "But now, let him who has a purse take it, and likewise a bag. And let him who has no sword sell his mantle and buy one. 37 For I tell you that this scripture must be fulfilled in me, 'And he was reckoned with transgressors'; for what is written about me has its fulfillment." 28 And they said, "Look, Lord, here are two swords." And he said to them, "It is enough."

CHAPTER 8

THE PASSION

At night Jesus and the disciples would go to the Mount of Olives just outside the city. And, as was his habit on so many former occasions, Jesus spends the night in prayer. The awful moment has arrived. He urges the disciples to pray; then taking his most intimate ones with him — Peter, James, and John — he goes apart to pray himself. Temptation is the key word here, for Jesus is besieged by doubt. Is a showdown with the authorities what the Heavenly Father wants him to do? His disciples are obviously not prepared to lead the New Israel. They are not ready to be the representatives of the kingdom on earth. Is this the time or would he not be deserting the very cause for which he had come into the world? And what about the Jerusalem he loved, the Jerusalem he had wept over? If he stayed now and faced his enemies, the Sanhedrin and the Holy City would undoubtedly have his blood on their hands. Should he permit himself to be the cause of their monstrous sin? Should he not slip away in the darkness and avoid it all? Rationalization. Temptation is rationalization — finding a good reason for not doing one's God-intended job.

Gethsemane was a spiritual battleground of world dimensions, and Peter and the others slept through it, later to succumb to temptation themselves.

22:39–46

39 And he came out, and went, as was his custom, to the Mount of Olives; and the disciples followed him.

40 And when he came to the place he said to them.
"Pray that you may not enter into temptation." 41 And
he withdrew from them about a stone's throw, and
knelt down and prayed, 42 "Father, if thou art willing,
remove this cup from me; nevertheless not my will, but
thine, be done."* 45 And when he rose from prayer, he
came to the disciples and found them sleeping for sor-
row, 46 and he said to them, "Why do you sleep? Rise
and pray that you may not enter into temptation."

*Other ancient authorities add verses 43 and 44: 43 And there ap-
peared to him an angel from heaven, strengthening him. 44 And
being in an agony he prayed more earnestly; and his sweat became
like great drops of blood falling down upon the ground.

The Arrest

The arresting party arrives, a hired mob, actually, including
some slaves who were not there through choice, all carrying clubs
and swords, with members of the Sanhedrin discreetly in the
background. It begins like a bad play. Judas identifies Jesus with
a kiss, awkwardly insincere. Then one of the disciples takes an in-
decisive swipe at the arresting bunch with his sword. Jesus
rebukes him; then over the heads of his captors he speaks to the
Sanhedrin members in the shadows, people who needed no help
from Judas to identify their arch-enemy: "I was with you day
after day in the temple." A legal arrest would have taken place
openly. This is happening under cover of darkness because it is
the work of the prince of darkness. The spiritual battle with the
Light of the World had now been joined.

22:47–53

47 While he was still speaking there came a crowd,
and the man called Judas, one of the twelve, was leading them. He drew near to Jesus to kiss him; 48 but Jesus
said to him, "Judas, would you betray the Son of man
with a kiss?" 49 And when those who were about him

saw what would follow, they said, "Lord, shall we strike with the sword?" 50 And one of them struck the slave of the high priest and cut off his right ear. 51 But Jesus said, "No more of this!" And he touched his ear and healed him. 52 Then Jesus said to the chief priests and officers of the temple and elders, who had come out against him, "Have you come out as against a robber, with swords and clubs? 53 When I was with you day after day in the temple, you did not lay hands on me. But this is your hour, and the power of darkness."

Peter's Denial

Luke crowds the trial of Jesus into a matter of hours. The late evening-early morning time in the high priest's house provides the setting for the soldiers' cruel buffoonery and Peter's denial. Perhaps no phrase in the Gospel is more charged with feeling than, "And the Lord turned and looked at Peter. And Peter remembered." He is the only disciple named in the Last Supper account. (Luke does not even bother to tell us that the others faded into the night after Jesus' arrest.) And he is the only disciple named in the resurrection appearances. Peter's spiritual agony and his ultimate authority in the early days of the Christian Church are carefully noted by Luke.

22:54–65

54 Then they seized him and led him away, bringing him into the high priest's house. Peter followed at a distance; 55 and when they had kindled a fire in the middle of the courtyard and sat down together, Peter sat among them. 56 Then a maid, seeing him as he sat in the light and gazing at him said, "This man also was with him." 57 But he denied it, saying, "Woman, I do not know him." 58 And a little later some one else saw him and said, "You also are one of them." But Peter

said, "Man, I am not." 59 And after an interval of about an hour still another insisted, saying, "Certainly this man also was with him; for he is a Galilean." 60 But Peter said, "Man, I do not know what you are saying." And immediately, while he was still speaking, the cock crowed. 61 And the Lord turned and looked at Peter. And Peter remembered the word of the Lord, how he had said to him, "Before the cock crows today, you will deny me three times." 62 And he went out, and wept bitterly.

63 Now the men who were holding Jesus mocked him and beat him; 64 they also blindfolded him and asked him, "Prophesy! Who is it that struck you?" 65 And they spoke many other words against him, reviling him.

The Trial

The succession of events called a "trial" was like a powerful motorboat driven by the Sanhedrin members which left a wake of uncomfortable, guilty people. There were some reputable men among the seventy members of the Sanhedrin. Some of them — like Nicodemus and Joseph of Arimathea — were certainly uncomfortable at the twisted political charges against Jesus which their leaders took to Pilate. Pilate had political insights into the motives of people who came into his court; he was no fool. He knew Jesus was innocent and he must have been uncomfortable with the travesty of justice he ultimately permitted. And Herod? He was not a profound man. He had gotten rid of troublesome John the Baptist in his heavy-handed way. This Jesus, like John but different, made him uncomfortable with his silence. Cruel humor is the face-saving cover-up of frustrated bullies. There were even uncomfortable folk in the shouting crowd. They were trapped in the Sanhedrin's evil orchestrations and did not have the courage to be conspicuous. (Notice the sorrowing crowd, 23:27,48.) Evil makes people uncomfortably guilty when they cannot find the courage to resist it. The "trial" was a black scene of monstrous evil, and for many it was made worse by the pervasive fog of their guilty share in it.

22:66–71

66 When day came, the assembly of the elders of the people gathered together, both chief priests and scribes; and they led him away to their council, and they said, 67 "If you are the Christ, tell us." But he said to them, "If I tell you, you will not believe; 68 and if I ask you, you will not answer. 69 But from now on the Son of man shall be seated at the right hand of the power of God." 70 And they all said, "Are you the Son of God, then?" And he said to them, "You say that I am." 71 And they said, "What further testimony do we need? We have heard it ourselves from his own lips."

23:1–25

Then the whole company of them arose, and brought him before Pilate. 2 And they began to accuse him, saying, "We found this man perverting our nation, and forbidding us to give tribute to Caesar, and saying that he himself is Christ a king." 3 And Pilate asked him, "Are you the King of the Jews?" And he answered him, "You have said so." 4 And Pilate said to the chief priests and the multitudes, "I find no crime in this man." 5 But they were urgent, saying, "He stirs up the people, teaching throughout all Judea, from Galilee even to this place."

6 When Pilate heard this, he asked whether the man was a Galilean. 7 And when he learned that he belonged to Herod's jurisdiction, he sent him over to Herod, who was himself in Jerusalem at that time. 8 When Herod saw Jesus, he was very glad, for he had long desired to see him, because he had heard about him, and he was hoping to see some sign done by him. 9 So he questioned

him at some length; but he made no answer. 10 The chief priests and the scribes stood by, vehemently accusing him. 11 And Herod with his soldiers treated him with contempt and mocked him; then, arraying him in gorgeous apparel, he sent him back to Pilate. 12 And Herod and Pilate became friends with each other that very day, for before this they had been at enmity with each other.

13 Pilate then called together the chief priest and the rulers and the people, 14 and said to them, "You brought me this man as one who was perverting the people; and after examining him before you, behold, I did not find this man guilty of any of your charges against him; 15 neither did Herod, for he sent him back to us. Behold, nothing deserving death has been done by him; 16 I will therefore chastise him and release him."*

18 But they all cried out together, "Away with this man, and release to us Barabbas" — 19 a man who had been thrown into prison for an insurrection started in the city, and for murder. 20 Pilate addressed them once more, desiring to release Jesus; 21 but they shouted out, "Crucify, crucify him!" 22 A third time he said to them, "Why, what evil has he done? I have found in him no crime deserving death; I will therefore chastise him and release him." 23 But they were urgent, demanding with loud cries that he should be crucified. And their voices prevailed. 24 So Pilate gave sentence that their demand should be granted. 25 He released the man who had been thrown into prison for insurrection and murder, whom they asked for; but Jesus he delivered up to their will.

*Here or after verse 19, some ancient authorities add verse 17, *Now he was obliged to release one man to them at the festival.*

Notice that in the questions the chief priests and their colleagues addressed to Jesus they identify the Christ (Messiah) with the Son of God. Luke has been at pains throughout his Gospel to make it clear that Jesus is Christ the Son of God and now even his enemies bear witness to that fact.

The irony of Jesus' trial lies in its duplicity; it is at every point the opposite of what it seems. The Sanhedrin thought they were judging Jesus, yet he reminds the court that he rather than they is the ultimate judge. For the Son of man will be given authority by God both to rule and to judge (22:69 and Dan. 7:13 f). Jesus was always at pains to avoid being a political Messiah, yet that was the only charge leveled at him before Pilate. Jesus the innocent is condemned for sedition while Barabbas, guilty of sedition, is released. Pilate, the representative of Roman justice, makes it a travesty. Truth and right and justice were all unseated that day. It was only with the eyes of faith that the Son of man was able to see that "his kingdom shall not be destroyed" (Dan. 7:14).

The Crucifixion

The awareness of the early Church that Jesus the Messiah was the Suffering Servant the Old Testament described made it natural (perhaps inevitable) to think of the events of his passion in scriptural terms. Allusions to the vicarious suffering of Isaiah's Servant of the Lord (Isa. 52:13-53:12) lie behind the whole account, as do quotations from the Psalms. The parting of his clothes and the scoffing echo Psalm 22:7, 18; the gift of vinegar is found in Psalm 69:21. Also the account is filled with much intended symbolism. None of this can be or should be peeled away. However, awareness of it helps us realize that we are viewing what took place through the eyes of faith and perhaps we should be on our knees, as Luke was figuratively on his as he wrote the account.

Jesus urges the sorrowing multitude to mourn, not for him, but for what was happening to their Holy City and to their nation. During perhaps the most painful moments of the crucifixion ordeal Jesus prayerfully reaches out in forgiving love. For whom is he praying? It is ambiguous. You write your own script about the extent of the Lord's caring. It is interesting that the mocking titles hurled at him all identify him as the Messiah — "Christ," "Chosen One," "King." And the Messiah reaches out to the thief on the adjacent cross, the kind of disinherited person he had always reached out to during his ministry. We do not know what the man expected from Jesus, but Jesus' promise is out of all proportion to his request.

It was a widespread belief in antiquity that in great and tragic moments the natural world showed its sympathy for the distress humans were suffering. That is the point of the detail about darkness. And the rent curtain in the Temple separating the Holy of Holies from the congregation symbolized new open access to the inner presence of God. As we said, the description is full of symbolism.

The comment of the Roman centurion that Jesus was innocent sums up a major Lucan theme — first Pilate, then the penitent thief, now the centurion. Isaiah's words had taken on flesh and blood:

Surely he has borne our griefs
and carried our sorrows;
yet we esteemed him stricken,
smitten by God, and afflicted.
But he was wounded for our transgressions. (Isa. 53:4-5)

The generous act of Joseph of Arimathea took great courage. It was a gesture which showed he was not in sympathy with the decision of the Sanhedrin. Whether he was a secret believer in Jesus is not clear (cf., John 3:1-12; 7:50-52; 19:39-41).

23:26-56

26 And as they led him away, they seized one Simon of Cyrene, who was coming in from the country, and laid on him the cross, to carry it behind Jesus. 27 And there followed him a great multitude of the people, and of women who bewailed and lamented him. 28 But Jesus turning to them said, "Daughters of Jerusalem, do not weep for me, but weep for yourselves and for your

children. 29 For behold, the days are coming when they will say, 'Blessed are the barren, and the wombs that never bore, and the breasts that never gave suck!' 30 Then they will begin to say to the mountains, 'Fall on us'; and to the hills, 'Cover us.' 31 For if they do this when the wood is green, what will happen when it is dry?"

32Two others also, who were criminals, were led away to be put to death with him. 33 And when they came to the place which is called The Skull, there they crucified him, and the criminals, one on the right and one on the left. 34 And Jesus said, "Father, forgive them; for they know not what they do." And they cast lots to divide his garments. 35 And the people stood by, watching; but the rulers scoffed at him, saying, "He saved others; let him save himself, if he is the Christ of God, his Chosen One!" 36 The soldiers also mocked him, coming up and offering him vinegar, 37 and saying, "If you are the King of the Jews, save yourself!" 38 There was also an inscription over him, "This is the King of the Jews."

39 One of the criminals who were hanged railed at him, saying, "Are you not the Christ? Save yourself and us!" 40 But the other rebuked him, saying, "Do you not fear God, since you are under the same sentence of condemnation? 41 And we indeed justly; for we are receiving the due reward of our deeds; but this man has done nothing wrong." 42 And he said, "Jesus, remember me when you come into your kingdom." 43 And he said to him, "Truly, I say to you, today you will be with me in Paradise."

44 It was now about the sixth hour, and there was darkness over the whole land until the ninth hour, 45 while the sun's light failed; and the curtain of the temple was torn in two. 46 Then Jesus, crying with a loud voice, said, "Father, into thy hands I commit my

spirit!" And having said this he breathed his last. 47 Now when the centurion saw what had taken place, he praised God, and said, "Certainly this man was innocent!" 48 And all the multitudes who assembled to see the sight, when they saw what had taken place, returned home beating their breasts. 49 And all his acquaintances and the women who had followed him from Galilee stood at a distance and saw these things.

50 Now there was a man named Joseph from the Jewish town of Arimathea. He was a member of the council, a good and righteous man, 51 who had not consented to their purpose and deed, and he was looking for the kingdom of God. 52 This man went to Pilate and asked for the body of Jesus. 53 Then he took it down and wrapped it in a linen shroud, and laid him in a rock-hewn tomb, where no one had ever yet been laid. 54 It was the day of Preparation, and the sabbath was beginning. 55 The women who had come with him from Galilee followed, and saw the tomb, and how his body was laid; 56 then they returned, and prepared spices and ointments.

On the sabbath they rested according to the commandment.

What happened at "the place which is called The Skull" exposes us to a kaleidoscope of attitudes toward Jesus. There is the vulgar curiosity of the crowd, the contemptuous derision of the rulers, the callous frivolity of the guard, and the bitter invective of the criminal. There is also the penitent thief's open awareness of something indescribable and the centurion's awe in the presence of sheer goodness. In the midst of these ripples of reaching and tension, of hostility, indifference, and awe, there is from Jesus a ground swell of caring, forgiveness, and love. "He is the image of the invisible God," wrote Paul a generation later (Col. 1:15).

CHAPTER 9

THE RESURRECTION

The resurrection of Jesus is a momentous event which is interlaced with the feelings and beliefs of the persons who were intimately involved. The record which has come down to us reached its present form about two generations after the crucifixion-resurrection, and was based on the written materials and oral traditions Luke had gathered. His analysis of these materials and his theological point of view about the crucified and risen Lord and about the Church and its mission colored his version of the resurrection record. Do not do Luke the injustice of treating his story of the resurrection as though it were a court reporter's documentary.

The Empty Tomb

Several facts stand out. In all four gospels Mary Magdalene is the first to spread the news that Jesus has risen and is alive. Luke is careful to make clear that this amazing fact has from the very first authentic apostolic endorsement. Some manuscripts add that endorsement here, stating that Peter, the leading apostle, was early at the tomb (see footnote, vs. 12), but probably the oldest bit of resurrection reporting is the statement, "The Lord has risen indeed, and has appeared to Simon" (23:34; see also I Cor. 15:5). Luke is saying to his readers that the event has validity based on apostolic testimony.

The empty tomb is a resurrection detail which seems to loom larger in importance than it really is. The earliest resurrection account is by Paul (I Cor. 15:3-8), at least two decades before Luke wrote. He makes no mention of the empty tomb. Except for "the disciple" (usually called "the Beloved Disciple") in John's Gospel (20:8), no New Testament person is said to have believed Jesus to be alive because the tomb was empty. The episode of the empty tomb is only a prologue, but is usually thought to be a necessary prologue, to belief in the resurrection.

In Luke, the initial realization that the Lord had risen from the dead came as such a surprise that the account is bereft of any indications of how the women felt. In Matthew, they hurried to tell the disciples "with fear and great joy" (Mt. 28:8). In Mark, they were dumbfounded — "afraid" and silent (Mk. 16:8). In John, Mary Magdalene, thinking the body had been removed, is upset and weeping (Jn. 20:11, 15). But Luke merely tells the stark details: an empty tomb, a vision of angels, and haste to report to the eleven who receive the news dubiously.

24:1-11

But on the first day of the week, at early dawn, they went to the tomb, taking spices which they had prepared. 2 And they found the stone rolled away from the tomb, 3 but when they went in they did not find the body. 4 While they were perplexed about this, behold, two men stood by them in dazzling apparel; 5 and as they were frightened and bowed their faces to the ground, the men said to them, "Why do you seek the living among the dead? 6 Remember how he told you, while he was still in Galilee, 7 that the Son of man must be delivered into the hands of sinful men, and be crucified, and on the third day rise." 8 And they remembered his words, 9 and returning from the tomb they told all this to the eleven and to all the rest. 10 Now it was Mary Magdalene and Joanna and Mary the mother of James and the other women with them who told this to the apostles; 11 but these words seemed to them an idle tale, and they did not believe them.*

*Some ancient authorities add verse 12, *But Peter rose and ran to the tomb; stooping and looking in, he saw the linen cloths by themselves; and he went home wondering at what had happened.*

On the Road to Emmaus

The story of the Risen Lord appearing to the couple en route to Emmaus on Easter Day is a literary gem. It is another good example of Luke's masterful storytelling with its vivid human touches. In the course of it the experience of the women at the empty tomb is briefly summarized. Notice that there is no hint now that the women's report was questioned or not accepted. The details suggest that the account was composed with an eye toward giving support to the embryo Christian Church. For instance, the statements about Jesus Christ sound much like the almost credal statements about him in the speeches in Acts (24:19-20, 26; cf. Acts 2:22-23; 10:37-39). What he is described as doing at their meal together — "he took the bread and blessed, and broke it, and gave it to them" (24:30; cf. 22:19) — is identical with what he did at the Last Supper and evidently at other meals. This meal and the interpreting of Scriptures were the ways in which the Church of Luke's day and since has continued to know the presence of the Risen Lord.

24:13–35

13 That very day two of them were going to a village named Emmaus, about seven miles from Jerusalem, 14 and talking with each other about all these things that had happened. 15 While they were talking and discussing together, Jesus himself drew near and went with them. 16 But their eyes were kept from recognizing him. 17 And he said to them, "What is this conversation which you are holding with each other as you

walk?" And they stood still, looking sad. 18 Then one of them, named Cleopas, answered him, "Are you the only visitor to Jerusalem who does not know the things that have happened there in these days?" 19 And he said to them, "What things?" And they said to him, "Concerning Jesus of Nazareth, who was a prophet mighty in deed and word before God and all the people, 20 and how our chief priests and rulers delivered him up to be condemned to death and crucified him. 21 But we had hoped that he was the one to redeem Israel. Yes, and besides all this, it is now the third day since this happened. 22 Moreover, some women of our company amazed us. They were at the tomb early in the morning 23 and did not find his body; and they came back saying that they had even seen a vision of angels, who said that he was alive. 24 Some of those who were with us went to the tomb, and found it just as the women had said; but him they did not see." 25 And he said to them, "O foolish men, and slow of heart to believe all that the prophets have spoken! 26 Was it not necessary that the Christ should suffer these things and enter into his glory?" 27 And beginning with Moses and all the prophets, he interpreted to them in all the scriptures the things concerning himself.

28 So they drew near to the village to which they were going. He appeared to be going further, 29 but they constrained him, saying, "Stay with us, for it is toward evening and the day is now far spent." So he went in to stay with them. 30 When he was at table with them, he took the bread and blessed, and broke it, and gave it to them. 31 And their eyes were opened and they recognized him; and he vanished out of their sight. 32 They said to each other. "Did not our hearts burn within us while he talked to us on the road, while he opened to us the scriptures?" 33 And they rose that same hour and returned to Jerusalem; and they found the eleven gath-

ered together and those who were with them, 34 who said, "The Lord has risen indeed, and has appeared to Simon!" 35 Then they told what had happened on the road, and how he was known to them in the breaking of the bread.

The Emmaus story was probably part of a collection of resurrection appearance accounts before it came into Luke's hands. He, however, refashioned it as a bridge, a transition piece. It not only looks back to the women and Peter at the empty tomb, but also to the Lord's passion and the fact that "all the scriptures" looked forward to the events which have now taken place. The story also looks toward the future. The Emmaus couple return to Jerusalem to tell the assembled apostles what has happened, and discover that the Risen Lord has also appeared to Peter. What will this unexpectedly revitalized band of Jesus' former followers do now? The story piques our curiosity and anticipation. Luke's style has been the same throughout. This last transition piece leads the reader toward his second volume, The Book of the Acts.

"You are Witnesses of These Things"

After the Emmaus couple have rejoined the apostolic gathering the Risen Lord appears in their midst. (The occasion is very similar to that described in John 20:19-23.) He shows them his scarred hands and feet and invites them to touch him in order to prove he is not a ghost. He eats with them for the same reason. This strong emphasis on the Lord's bodily resurrection is a reaction to the pressures of the times in which Luke composed his Gospel.

As the Christian Church developed and spread into Greek-speaking areas of the Roman world distorted views of the nature of Jesus Christ began to appear. One of these, Docetism, contended that Jesus was a divine being who only seemed to be human. He had not actually become a man, suffered, and died. The Church was at great pains to establish the fact that he was truly man as well as truly God. This distortion of Christian belief about

Jesus (historical vandalism, really) did not exist prominently in the early years of the Church. But when Luke wrote and when the Fourth Gospel was written this tendency to consider the resurrected Lord a ghost had to be combated with proof of his resurrected physical bodiness (Jn. 20:20). Hence his insistence that they both inspect his crucifixion wounds and touch him; and his act of eating in their presence.

The significance of this second resurrection appearance lies in the fact that it supplies that which was missing in the initial appearance: what believers were supposed to do. At this second appearance the Risen Lord supplies that lack. He first lays a spiritual foundation. "All the scriptures" — Moses, the prophets, the Psalms — looked toward the coming of the Christ who was to suffer, die, and rise again. It is the message of which the women at the tomb had been reminded, and which the Risen Lord has explained earlier to the Emmaus travelers. Then he charges them to go forth as his witnesses and preach repentance and forgiveness in his Name to "all nations." First, however, they must wait in Jerusalem until the Risen Lord sends them "power from on high," his Spirit.

Then he blesses them and ascends into heaven.

24:36–53

36 As they were saying this, Jesus himself stood among them. 37 But they were startled and frightened, and supposed that they saw a spirit. 38 And he said to them, "Why are you troubled, and why do questionings rise in your hearts? 39 See my hands and my feet, that it is I myself; handle me, and see; for a spirit has not flesh and bones as you see that I have."* 41 And while they still disbelieved for joy, and wondered, he said to them, "Have you anything here to eat?" 42 They gave him a piece of broiled fish, 43 and he took it and ate before them.

44 Then he said to them, "These are my words which I

spoke to you, while I was still with you, that everything written about me in the law of Moses and the prophets and the psalms must be fulfilled." 45 Then he opened their minds to understand the scriptures, 46 and said to them, "Thus it is written, that the Christ should suffer and on the third day rise from the dead, 47 and that repentance and forgiveness of sins should be preached in his name to all nations, beginning from Jerusalem. 48 You are witnesses of these things. 49 And behold, I send the promise of my Father upon you; but stay in the city, until you are clothed with power from on high."

50 Then he led them out as far as Bethany, and lifting up his hands he blessed them. 51 While he blessed them, he parted from them, and was carried up into heaven. 52 And they returned to Jerusalem with great joy, 53 and were continually in the temple blessing God.

*Some ancient authorities add verse 40, *And when he had said this, he showed them his hands and his feet.*

Luke thinks of the apostles as "witnesses of these things" (see Acts 1:8 and 22), meaning of the ministry, death, resurrection, and ascension of Jesus. The intent of this message is to bring about repentance and forgiveness of sins.

In Luke's conception of salvation history Jerusalem is the center from which the message of salvation will spread to "all nations." Consequently, he establishes Jerusalem and vicinity as the locale of the resurrection appearances. Jesus was from Galilee and the disciples were Galileans. In both Matthew and Mark the angel at the tomb sent word to the disciples that the Risen Lord would meet them in Galilee. Not so in Luke. For him Galilee is a thing of the past to be remembered. Jerusalem is now the center from which (in his next book) the Gospel will go out to the world.

Jerusalem is the center because it is the locale of the Temple which is the spiritual center of Israel. That is why Jesus' official visit to the Holy City (19:41–44) is of such great importance. The

Christ has come to offer salvation to Israel. By the same token, that is why the rejection of Jesus in Jerusalem is the more grievous.

The Temple is the heart of Jerusalem, so Luke begins and ends his Gospel in the Temple. Zechariah is performing his priestly liturgy in the Temple when the Gospel opens. Jesus lifts his hands in a typically priest-like way when he blesses the apostles just before he ascends, and they are in the Temple joyfully praising God when the Gospel closes.

The ascension of the Risen Lord is for Luke the climax of his Gospel. Jesus' death on the cross and his resurrection are necessary stepping stones to his being received up in glory. As the Lord explained to the couple on the Emmaus road, "It was necessary that the Christ should suffer these things and *enter into his glory*" (24:26). His going up to Jerusalem was in order "to be received up" (9:51). The indispensable preliminary to that exaltation is his death and resurrection, seen as a single event by which his glorification is accomplished (12:50; 13:32 f). For Luke the resurrection is not an end in itself or a symbol of the Lord's final victory, but a point of transition. It looks to what will follow—the gift of the Spirit and the mission of the Church. It also looks back on that firm scriptural base which helps give appreciation to the life, death, and resurrection of Jesus. For the Lord's followers the period of the resurrection appearances is temporary and is brought to an end by his ascension into heaven, which is a prelude to the era of the Spirit. For this reason, the Ascension, the pivotal event, is both the final happening of Luke's Gospel and the opening incident of the Book of Acts—the narrative of the Spirit-empowered Church proclaiming the Gospel from Jerusalem to Samaria to Rome.

CHAPTER 10

A FINAL LOOK

In the scenario of salvation, Christ the Savior is born. Imbued with the Holy Spirit he takes up his ministry. He proclaims the presence of the kingdom of God in his conquest of the powers of evil in all its forms — sickness, demonic possession, sin, and death. The leaders of Israel fill their historic role of rejecting him as their forebears had rejected the prophets before them. Thus they deny "the purpose of God" (7:30). But that purpose is not to be set aside. It has a glacier-like irresistibility as it moves toward fulfillment. Jesus recognizes this. "We are going up to Jerusalem," he tells the Twelve, "and everything that is written of the Son of man *will be accomplished*" (18:31). On that first Easter morning the angels at the tomb remind the women that Jesus had told them "that the Son of man *must be* delivered into the hands of sinful men, and be crucified, and on the third day rise" (24:7). And the Risen Lord explains both to the couple on the road to Emmaus and to the later gathering of the apostles that "all the scriptures" foretold his death and resurrection as fulfilling "Moses and the prophets" and as being *"necessary"* (24:25-27, 44-46). So all through the story of Jesus we sense an inexorable unstoppableness of movement toward the divine intention.

This impressive tide of divine purpose does not end with what happened to Jesus. The Risen Lord's final word to the apostles before his Ascension was that "You are witness of these things," and that this message of the saving power of God should be preached to "all nations" (24:47-48). The parallel account of the

Lord's final words before his Ascension in the opening of the Book of Acts makes even more imperative the response of those faithful to the Risen Lord: "You shall receive power when the Holy Spirit has come upon you; and *you shall be my witnesses* . . . to the end of the earth" (Acts 1:8). Luke intends that not only the apostles but all who identify themselves with the Risen Lord consider themselves to be under an inescapable divine authority like that of the earthly Jesus.

The meaning of salvation to Luke is that it involves accepting the new life of healing and pardon which the Lord offers, and also accepting his ensuing demand, "Take up your cross daily and follow me . . . whoever loses his life for my sake, he will save it" (9:23-24).

Luke does not intend that his readers should sit on the sidelines.

BIBLIOGRAPHY

A host of books on Luke's Gospel or aspects of it have of late and through the years contributed to my thinking on this subject. Here are the ones which have been most helpful in preparing this monograph.

Raymond E. Brown, *The Birth of the Messiah: A Commentary on the Infancy Narratives in Matthew and Luke.* Garden City, N. Y.: Doubleday, 1977.

G. B. Caird, *The Gospel of St. Luke.* The Penguin New Testament Commentary series. Baltimore, Md.: Penguin Books, 1963.

Hans Conzelmann, *The Theology of Luke.* New York: Harper & Row, 1961.

E. Earle Ellis, *The Gospel of Luke.* The Century Bible (new edition). London: Thomas Nelson & Sons, Ltd., 1966.

C. F. Evans, *Resurrection and the New Testament.* Studies in Biblical Theology, Second series, 12. Naperville, Ill.: Alec R. Allenson Inc., 1970.

Reginald H. Fuller, *The Formation of the Resurrection Narratives.* New York: Macmillan Co., 1971.

Jack Dean Kingsbury, *Jesus Christ in Matthew, Mark, and Luke.* Proclamation Commentaries series. Philadelphia: Fortress Press, 1981.

Chas. M. Laymon, *The Interpreter's One-Volume Commentary on the Bible.* New York: Abingdon Press, 1971.

I. Howard Marshall, *The Gospel of Luke: A Commentary on the Greek Text.* The New International Greek Commentary series. Grand Rapids, Mich.: Wm. B. Eerdmans Publishing Co., 1978.

James Luther Mays (ed.), *Interpreting the Gospels.* Philadelphia: Fortress Press, 1981.

Paul S. Minear, *The Interpreter and the Birth Narratives.* Symbolae Biblicae Upsalienses, 13. Uppsala: Wretmans Boktryckeri A.-B., 1950.

Edward Schillebeeckx, *Jesus: An Experiment in Christology.* A Crossroad Book. New York: The Seabury Press, 1979.